# EMBRACING GRACE

## What Spiritual Leaders Say About *Embracing Grace*:

"The tension between grace and performance, though so foundational to our faith, has baffled many for far too long. Like a major 7th, it begs to be resolved. Daniel Brown grapples with this tension, like Jacob in Genesis 32, and artfully engages us in the wrestling match along with him. *Embracing Grace* is a masterful consideration of all the elements in the equation of the Law and Grace. Echoing Jacob's "until you bless me," Brown does not let go until his readers grasp truths and find blessings long obscured by fear, self-reproach, and legalism."

*Wayne Cordeiro, Senior Pastor, New Hope Christian Fellowship, Honolulu, HI, Author of* Simply Jesus *and* Leading on Empty

"How you define a word determines how you live. That's why people sometimes hijack the meanings of words—so they can reshape truth to fit their agenda. That is certainly true of the word 'grace.' Ever since New Testament times, a war has raged over this powerful word. Grace, when understood correctly, is the doorway to a rich and intimate relationship with God. When twisted and misunderstood, however, it can lead to deception.

"Because there are plenty of hijackers at work today, including well-meaning people who want to turn grace into something it was never meant to be, I've been suspicious of many recently published books discussing our guilt, and God's love and forgiveness. So, I was thrilled my friend Daniel Brown decided to explain this incredible but misunderstood truth.

"I trust him not only as a mentor, but also as a skilled handler of God's Word. Daniel Brown is not a hijacker. He carefully balances the truths of Scripture, so that nothing gets twisted or uneven. He has lived a life of grace; you'll sense that in his simple, scriptural, and non-religious language. I pray that many people will embrace God's grace in a fresh way after reading this important book."

*J. Lee Grady, Contributing Editor,* Charisma
*Author, Director of* The Mordecai Project

"Why do we equate righteousness with our works and unrighteousness with our sins? As Daniel Brown explains in this excellent, to-the-point book, many believers struggle to be right with God, and miss the fact that God made us right with Him.

"Daniel eloquently displays the difference between that voice which condemns believers, and that which tells us we are accepted in God by faith, alone. His illustrations intrigued me, as did his short cruise through scripture. This book is a keeper for anyone struggling with an accusing conscience."

*Ralph Moore, Founder of Hope Chapels*
*Author of* Defeating Anxiety

"As I read this compelling story that started with a confrontation by a self-appointed prophet in Greece, I became more convinced that I also hear the judgments of the enemy against my soul. Who among us hasn't been subject to the *Spirit of the Pharisee* that accuses us of denying the faith every time we sin?

"Reading this book will be like hiring a contractor to come into your home to remodel . . . first by demolition of walls that need to come down, and then by building up who we really are by *embracing grace*."

*Peter Bonanno, Lead Pastor, Grace Capital Church, Pembroke, NH*

"What a great piece of doctrinal and pragmatic work. Outstanding! *Embracing Grace* masterfully describes both the never-ending-guilt assault that every believer endures, and how we can access God's impenetrable fortress of grace. My weapon belt is now much better equipped to fight off legalism and condemnation. Never before have I read a more thorough, scripturally sound and practically relevant explanation of Law vs. Grace. Daniel's detailed perspectives—so loaded with intriguing biblical texts, yet so easy to read—have given me numerous practical insights for counseling.

"This book gives us the language to explain one of the believer's biggest problems, and how to access the solution provided through Christ Jesus. Dr. Brown includes many additional insights on Kingdom life. I especially appreciate his insights about "false personas," and the way he describes—actually exposes—the intentional enemy's plot to embed false identity traits into a person, and then influence that person to accept them as original and permanent."

*Jerry D. Dirmann, Lead Pastor, The Rock, Anaheim, CA*

"'You are not under the law, but under grace' (Romans 6:14) is an amazing concept, the implications of which we are often reticent to explore. In *Embracing Grace*, Daniel Brown explores this truth with unabashed candor and insight, offering practical and pastoral insights that are certain to help Christ-followers navigate the maze of 'being forgiven' vs. 'being good.'

"Though following in the tradition of centuries of Church scholars, what he says is certain to challenge and possibly even upset many . . . but the challenge is worth it because of its promise for a potentially revolutionized personal experience with Christ."

*Gary Matsdorf, MA, Executive Director,*
*New Hope Christian College, Eugene, OR*

"What a remarkable and thorough work on grace! I've admired 'Dr. Brown' for years. But knowing 'Daniel' for the past three years and observing his words, mannerisms, and speech, it doesn't surprise me that he would write a book about God's grace. *Embracing Grace* takes the complexities and seeming contradictions of grace and places them—like cookies—on the lower shelf.

"Daniel simplifies and clarifies the centuries old tug-of-war that yanks Christians back and forth: "Have I truly been forgiven?" and "Why do I feel as though I am not, and have to earn it back?" You will—at least, I did—breathe sighs of relief and realization as each turned page draws you to the next.

"Point by point, Daniel answers nagging questions and exposes the lies in 'religious thinking.' *Embracing Grace* should be read by anyone wanting true freedom in Christ put in plain words."

*Mike Kai, Lead Pastor, Hope Chapel West Oahu, HI*
*Author of* The Pound for Pound Principle

"Growing up in a legalistic household where the 'dos and don'ts' were front and center, I lived under a cloud of self-imposed failure. Although I tried desperately to keep all the rules, I felt I just couldn't measure up to God's expectations. Don't get me wrong, I knew God loved me, but in the end, my failures outweighed the truth of His love, and I was left feeling that God disapproved of me. *Embracing Grace* is a powerful book on the depth of God's grace, mercy, and promises for believers.

"As I read the pages I secretly wished that I could have read them 25 years ago . . . what a difference this revelation would have made. If your desire is to break the cloud of failure and legalism over your life, I encourage you to read the truths found in these pages. You will be forever changed and freed to live in a relationship with a God who passionately loves and embraces you."

*Juniece Fillingham, Co-lead Pastor, The Bridge,*
*Christiansburg, VA*

"Daniel Brown's *Embracing Grace* allows God's kindness in Jesus to settle deeper still in our theology and lifestyle. There are many voices aiding us in grace—yet Daniel's rings with vibrant honesty and creative study. I have walked out a relationship with Jesus ever mindful of looming brokenness that just won't quite go away. In *Embracing Grace*, I was reminded that I truly am a child of God, no longer a rebel, and by His kindness and power toward me, I am able to live out the message of Jesus I have believed."

*Chris Manginelli, Lead Pastor, Mill Creek Church,*
*Mill Creek, WA*

"This book is for the common man like myself as it answers the questions so many Christians have about Grace vs. Law in real-life situations. With an international perspective, and yet a very personal approach, Daniel tackles topics that I deal with in a very real way on a daily basis. His chapter on 'Why the Law?' addresses many nagging concerns I have had as to what is the point of the Old Testament—especially since Jesus said

He didn't come to abolish the Law, but seemed to change a lot of it. This is a must read for this current time!"

*Joseph Fehlen, Author of* Ride On,
*Rhinelander, WI*

"*Embracing Grace* convicted me about how familiar the 'voice of the Law' is in my spiritual life. It enlightened me to see all the ways I try to earn God's love and grace, and inspired me to believe I'm more loved and accepted by God than I could ever imagine."

*Kelly Tshibaka, JD, Washington, D.C.,*
*Creator of the* This Is Discipling *video*

"As a pastor, missionary, mentor, and friend, Dr. Daniel Brown tackles the tough and often touchy subject of grace in this brave new book. Challenging my conceptions, he drove me to the Word of God where I found that not all I thought I knew about Grace and the Law is correct. My congregation and I have already been impacted by this game-changing book!"

*Darin C. Stambaugh, Lead Pastor, Wooster Foursquare Church,*
*Wooster, Ohio*

"While every believer proclaims the joys of forgiveness, the reality is that many of us struggle with guilt and shame. Some of us can quote verses and explain why we shouldn't feel that way, but we still feel distant from God. With thought-provoking personal stories and insights that help make sense of the whole narrative of Scripture, Daniel Brown has written a book that can help restore intimacy with God.

"It's deep, it's practical, and it's personal. I could say it's a page-turner, but more to-the-point is how God will leaf through the pages of your heart, reworking your understanding of your own story, so that you can experience His love and grace down to the core of your being."

*Todd Millikan, Co-lead Pastor,*
*The Coastlands. Aptos, CA*

"If you have ever wrestled the giants of guilt and condemnation, this book is for you. Dr. Brown's explanation of how the Law and Grace work together has brought new freedom and love into all of my relationships!"

*Jason Voelp, Evangelist, Mansfield, Ohio*

"Freedom from guilt is an essential topic for the church to communicate concisely. It comes up in many conversations that I have with people in our church. I am thankful that Dr. Daniel Brown has undertaken the task of illuminating this concept in an engaging way that the entire church will benefit from. Our hearts cry for freedom, and as we know the truth we can be free indeed!"

*Johnny Chapman, Lead Pastor, FrontRange Church,*
*Westminster, CO*

"Daniel Brown brings years of ministry experience and spiritual insight into a topic that has plagued the church and every believer for generations. In a clear and lucid style he uncovers the trap that is legalism, and provides a road map to the freedom and grace Jesus intends for us all. Every believer should read this book."

*Daniel Lawrie, Lead Pastor, His Way Community Church,*
*Valencia, CA*

"This is the most balanced and thorough explanation of grace—and the most freeing book—I have ever read. I want everyone I love to read it. Dr. Daniel Brown presents the concepts of grace, judgment, mercy, sin, forgiveness, eternal security in such a simple way that so much makes sense to me now.

"I kept asking myself, 'Why has no one taught me these truths before? I have been in ministry for almost twenty years, but I learned truths from *Embracing Grace* I wish I could have learned twenty years ago.'

"You have been warned: Dr. Brown's best book yet is not for wimps. It shook my world; it will shake yours, too, because he makes us look with new lenses at truths we thought we understood. I underlined so many portions that I ran out of highlighters. I'm one of the first to have my life changed by this book!"

*Jay M. Bean, Lead Pastor, Grace Chapel Church,*
*Springfield, MO*

"Dr. Brown's consistent ability to pierce through theological jargon and to touch the heart of the reader is what makes his books worthy of an audience. His writing is practical, deep, orthodox, and funny. I encourage you to enjoy *Embracing Grace* and to apply its wisdom."

*Russ Schlecht, Lead Pastor, Living Word Fellowship,*
*Oak Harbor, WA*

"Misunderstanding Law and Grace distorts our perspective of God—making Him distant and fuzzy—and not at all like the God described in the Bible. *Embracing Grace* clears your vision of God. It presents a simple but life-changing understanding of God's commands and promises, and of His Law and Grace. It is the truth that will set many free.

"Dr. Daniel Brown draws on an incredible number of Bible passages to clarify issues that have bothered believers for centuries. His unique writing style weaves all those scriptures seamlessly into his sentences, so you almost don't notice how many verses he uses."

*David Berry, Co-lead Pastor, The Worship Center,*
*South Boston, VA*

"I met Daniel Brown in my first year as a senior pastor, and I am so glad I did. He has this amazing ability to help Christ-followers think differently about familiar aspects of God. This book is no different. He takes the lid off of a large pot and stirs the soup of guiltiness, the Law and Grace—so we get the full flavor of true, guilt-defying grace."

*Abe Pfeifer, Lead Pastor, New Hope,*
*Salem, Oregon*

"Daniel has a remarkable way of simplifying complex truths of the Kingdom, so everyone understands them—differently than they did before! Whether you are a seasoned and mature Christ-follower or new to the faith, the truths unlocked in this book will greatly benefit you as you grow as a disciple and disciple others."

*Ryan and Holly Schlecht*
*Lead Pastors, Valley Foursquare Church, Duvall, WA*

"This is a clear call to walk in the freedom that the grace of God provides. Just when I think I've understood the meaning of grace, I'm surprised when I uncover new and beautiful layers. Dr. Brown has revealed truth that brings hope and draws me joyfully toward Jesus, my Advocate, my Champion, my Savior. I invite you to throw off the shackles of condemnation and legalism and find freedom in the Gospel."

*Anne Lawson, Co-lead Pastor, River of Life Church,*
*Berea, KY*

"Dr. Daniel Brown's exposition on the relationship between Grace and the Law/faith and works is clear, crisp, and compelling. Whether you are a theologian seeking an erudite commentary on the doctrine of grace, or a believer who is searching for a practical understanding of what it means to live as one who has been justified by grace, this book is a must read.

"Dr. Brown's seminal work has resolved my personal struggles with the Book of James and the relationship between Faith and Works. And it doubtless would have done the same for Martin Luther, had he been privileged to benefit from Dr. Brown's scholarship in this area.

"Our Righteous Judge has replaced His gavel with the Cross on which our Advocate was crucified. We have been found "Not Guilty," both now and forevermore. Thank you, Dr. Brown, for this book. It is a gift to the Church!"

*Niki Tshibaka, JD, Lead Pastor, MVFF,*
*Alexandria, VA*

# EMBRACING GRACE

## Settling the Guilt that Unsettles You

By Daniel A. Brown, PhD

Authentic

*Embracing Grace*
Copyright © 2013
Daniel A. Brown, PhD

Cover design by Dan Pitts

Published by Authentic Publishers
188 Front Street, Suite 116-44
Franklin, TN 37064
Authentic Publishers is a division of
Authentic Media, Inc.

Printed in the United States of America

**Library of Congress Cataloging-in-Publication Data**

Brown PhD, Daniel A.
Embracing grace : Settling the guilt that unsettles you / Daniel A. Brown
p. cm.

ISBN 978-1-78078-102-0
978-1-78078-202-7 (e-book)

# Acknowledgments

The process that led to this book spanned three years, and in that time a great many individuals helped craft and fine tune what I wanted to say. Without Pastor George Patsaouras and my friends in Athens, the episode that triggered my writing wouldn't have happened. My past and current assistants, Danielle Mueller, Lindsay Brown, and Kayli Catron, coordinated more than they should have needed to do—but they worked for a somewhat disorganized boss.

Special thanks, also, to my tireless, volunteer proofreader, Susie Courtney; I think she read the manuscript more times than I did. Kyle Duncan, my editor, gave me just the right amount of encouragement and freedom of choice to enable me to present truths creatively but clearly. He called himself my Sherpa, and just wanted me to get the book up the hill.

Several others read various versions along the way and offered incredibly helpful suggestions, and their torturous questions drove me to answer far more than I originally intended. Their realness prevented even the slightest Christian cliché: so we're all grateful to Kelly Tshibaka, Dave Mann, Judy Gonzales, Maria Marinos, Gail Jackson, Christina Eltrevoog, Katee Wangia, Evan Brown, Karin Albert, Madalin Passerino, Isaac Argel, and Brad King. Pamela, my wife, always makes my writing better.

To "Pastor Jack" Hayford,
foremost of his generation
to pass along truths of the Kingdom
to me and mine.
He taught me to draw deeply from God's Word.

# Table of Contents

# Foreword

It is a statistical fact that the most widely sung Christian hymn in the world is "Amazing Grace." That fact alone is enough to suggest the scope of reality lodged within the collective soul of the vastness of humanity. Anywhere that hymn is sung—and it rises in venues that otherwise would hardly have space for anything that hinted at spiritual interests—this song of "Grace" echoes our common, sensed need for God's embrace.

It resounds with the melodic resonance we, as believers, communally feel and express when we are reminded by a speaker, or join to sing any lyric that speaks of God's grace, love and forgiveness. Yet amid the flower and fame of "Amazing Grace," though its verses present an expanding testimony to the heart of God and His loving ways toward us, the song actually only *introduces* God's grace.

The book you have taken in hand is more than an introduction; it is an excursion—an expedition into the heart of God. If the vernacular of music were employed, it would be called more than a song—a full concerto, perhaps. The practical approach of *Embracing Grace* may reduce it's chance of being designated "a classic" at this time, but I predict it will shortly become a favorite of many believers, and that it will progressively find an increasing audience.

You are about to begin reading "a new song;" one that develops a time-less truth, but sets it to a fresh arrangement. This new arrangement brings out the glory of grace as though it were a concert played by a 60-piece orchestra, resound with the full symphonic beauty and reality contained in God's amazing grace.

The music analogy is apt here, because you are taking in hand a work which, indeed, succeeds in adjusting some "pop arrangements." These "arrangements" have either reduced the richness of God-the-Composer's original score, or have created dissonant counter-point themes that distort the magnificence of what Jesus' death meant for us at the Cross as He became the Author of our Salvation—the originator of The Song.

I propose that *Embracing Grace* is a book to first be read for your own edification; second, to be read periodically for personal refreshing; and third, to warmly recommend to others as well. I see its content as comparable to my playing a song recorded on a CD someone gave me, then finding I want to replay it again and again. Its content is not unlike a new song, both beautiful and happy—a hope-filled and holy song worthy of a replay now and then, and not just a single "spin."

This book will embrace *you*, and help you enter a deeper embrace as you better grasp the gift, wonder, and rest God's grace offers each of us. Read it all: it reveals all that Heaven's Heart provided for us: 1) foreknowing our loss, (2) foretelling His promise, and—in Christ—(3) supplying an overflow of loving-kindness; and (4) while answering our deepest longings, also meeting our deepest need with a divine "grace upon grace" (John 1:16 NKJV).

> *Saving grace*, that can cover our failures and will expunge our record of guilt.
>
> *Magnanimous grace*, that gives heaven's wealth of love without cost to us.
>
> *Liberating grace*, brings us freedom from the pit and snares that have:
>
> > Starved our souls and snagged us at our weakest points; and
> >
> > Stained our conscious and stunted our growth; or
> >
> > Stabbed our hopes to death, leaving only darkness before us.

In a word, God wants us to know His *fullness of grace*; not only a song with a few verses (though the lyrics of "Amazing Grace" *do* afford a classic prelude for the grandest chorale, anytime . . . anywhere!).

However, I am privileged to precede this well-conceived, insight-filled study; one I believe you will find "amazing" in its own way. My word choice is neither glib nor mere flattery: I'm not given to platitudes or exaggeration. But I do want to assert that I am deeply grateful for that expression of God's grace-gifting that has equipped Daniel Brown to write with the human sensitivity, sanctified scholarship, spiritual sanity, and practical sensibility evident in these pages.

*Embracing Grace* is thorough enough to be a comprehensive study, celebrative enough to awaken praise and rejoicing, and patient enough to creatively communicate in ways that will help each reader to "feel" the embrace of God's grace as well as "learn" of it. This book, with an accessible simplicity, calls us all into a deeper depth and devotion—a deepened gratitude and a *higher* devotion.

It prompts us unto a more joyous freedom, a more sobered humility, a more confident assurance and an obedience untainted by legalism, guilt, or mere duty. Grace, ever more fully embraced, will converge such responses in ways that are merited by the incalculable, indescribable glory of God's grace.

I have personally been blessed and edified while reading this book: I gladly confess to learning from a man who has warmly affirmed my having contributed to his life and thought. It is an added joy to find that any investment I may have made in Daniel is now returning dividends to me at a vastly higher rate of interest than my contribution would explain. I make this observation, however, to urge older leaders like me to remain "teachable."

Though I've preached, taught, and written much that has blessed others, my greater quest is to live openly before the Holy Spirit's call to know a life-long, ever-deepening transformation by God's Spirit of grace in my own life. That pursuit removes any possibility that I merely read these pages as a professional analyst or critic. Sixty-plus years as a follower of Jesus and fifty-plus years as a pastor-teacher in His Church have taught me to never forget that, first, I am one of the Great Shepherd's *sheep*, and that, second, I am called as a *pastor*—one of His under-shepherds. I need His daily leadings "in the paths of righteousness for His namesake"—and

His repeated "anointing [of the] head with oil," so the overflow of His Spirit will keep my "cup running over" with substance, freshness, and vitality being transmitted to those I lead. *Embracing Grace* has already become a resource toward that end.

So it was, as I read and fed on the truth and beauty this book delivered to me by my dear fellow-shepherd, Daniel Brown, that I was recurrently delighted to note *four things*: how *astutely, practically, squarely*, and *beautifully* this book presents "grace." Allow me to elaborate my reasons for those adverbs.

First, as you read, you will find the author *astutely stepping into your thoughts*; raising a question, defining a problem or providing an answer, just as you, the reader, begin to wonder about the exact things he addresses. You will also discover the skillful way he takes you through "long answers" in ways that avoid shallow shortcuts, yet never seem wearying as you make the journey with him. You will also find that Daniel partners with you, helping to identify the source of the not-so-subtle jabbering that sometimes echoes in your skull. Daniel exposes the whispers or shouts of our adversary as he argues propositions of "truth" that, being worse than lies, are fiery darts, targeted on your soul. That same enemy uses strategic weapons fashioned to detonate with discouragement, depression and defeat, striving to ignite a flow of "true lies" which God's grace has already rendered powerless, but which condemnation's rebuttals relentlessly insinuate upon you. Nonetheless, be at ease: you'll find the power of God's grace to retaliate with "the weapons of our warfare" (II Cor. 10:4,5); equipped in ways you'll find heartening as you read the pages to follow.

Second, as a pastor and teacher, I have always found the author to write and teach with a consistent focus on *practically illustrating* key points. You'll find yourself underlining words and phrases (bracketing whole paragraphs at times) with footnotes to yourself citing another *"how to"* you've been given. This derives from teaching that helps believers in Christ "know that *knowing* God" is not merely a mystical experience or a mental assembling of information for the sake of argument or brainwashing. Knowing the Truth is more than having the right information:

it is about another matter of "rights." As John 1:12 puts it, by our being born again, we have also been given "the right to become sons and daughters of God;" (that is, literally certified by God's throne to receive the privileged authority to live and grow in God's family as His very own offspring!). *How gloriously practical* that *is*; and *it's how all the Bible's truths are meant to be.* Thus, as you read, expect the Holy Spirit to enlarge your grasp of grace: the puzzle pieces will be sorted for you as you read. Your part is to take what is at hand—practical application that will bring you a *growth* in *and enjoyment* of *grace's benefit—here and NOW!* It's what the Holy Spirit does when the grandeur of grace becomes more than a slogan.

Third, I want to affirm how *squarely* the message in this book aligns with God's Word. While *Embracing Grace* is not a theological textbook, the author is certainly not a theological novice: neither is he a negligent teacher. *Everything written in Dr. Brown's treatise, and each truth discerned and presented within it, squarely aligns with the most exacting doctrine espoused by trustworthy evangelical scholars.* This worthy feature contrasts sharply with the looseness of some contemporary "hip and pop" preaching and writing about "grace."

There is a cavalier bent toward glibness when God's generosity is described; an ease with which a "casual" or "cute" approach glibly opens doors to confusion and error. Sadly, this either reflects a sloppiness in handling God's Word, or an indifference toward what hearers actually conclude. I am not arguing for a stogy-styled ministry, but for a worthy weight of delivery when teaching God's great truths of love, grace, forgiveness, and mercy.

My concerns are *not* related to anything in this book, nor to the host of faithful teachers and leaders who demonstrate a sobered sense of their duty as men and women who stand between the living and the dead. However, there resides a significant recklessness of speech and a "mass media, sound bite" style that tempts some: examples are as common as last Sunday's message at some locations, or telecast from last night's cheerleading session aired via Christian television. However clever or sincere such messengers may be, the thinness of their content—coining their sloganeered comments but seldom providing scripturally based *teaching*—

offers only loosely spoken phrases that "scratch itching ears" and garners either laughter or excitable "amens," while pouring little of substance into the spiritual foundations of those hearing them. The outcome is painfully predictable—hollow faith and shallow living.

*Embracing Grace* affords a stark contrast to the above: Great truths, graciously taught and carefully sown in the hearts and minds of hearers, will lead to personal stability, health, and fruitfulness. This is what is derived when the soul's root system is nurtured with such enriching content, as you will find here. It is immensely satisfying to read a book so interesting and accessible, but that also declares God's Word with wisdom—thoroughly taught, warmly ministered, and spiritually energizing.

The predictable outcome of teaching that *"squares with God's Word"* is that it grows believers who personally experience the very practical, present hope Paul described in Colossians 1:27. There, he speaks of believers just like you and me, being transformed within as Truth becomes a "living encounter with Jesus," transmitting into our own life experience *"the glorious secret now being known, which is Christ in you, the hope of glory!"* It's what it means to know Christ—to "have Jesus my Savior living in me"—as He keeps on setting us free and as He continues growing us up!

Fourth, and finally, I want to briefly observe: this book is *artfully and beautifully written.* I won't elaborate this point but it deserves mention: It's an appropriate feature seeing there is nothing more beautiful than the nature of the living God, whose being is the essence of love; whose laws and ways are always enveloped in mercy, justice and truth. The very God whose manner in all things is as great in grace, favor, and kindness as it is great in strength, power, and might. This book's theological foundation is structurally strong, sound, and grounded in God's truth, but in a tender, holy, and spiritual way. It is "painted" with a texture and tone, joined to a delicacy of expression at pivotal points, and touching with understanding and healing.

At other points, truth glimmers like a pool in the desert, inviting worn and wounded souls to the clean, clear, and cool waters of life, freely flowing and transforming our journey from a dead-end to one of living strength and hope. Thus, as you read, expect to capture flashes of the overwhelming beauty of God's graciousness at its fuller dimension and depth. It's radiance and splendor are increasingly awe-inspiring, I assure you.

With seventy-seven years of life behind me, I am still amazed at how I am amazed again and again. My most recent "amazement" was encountered in these pages. I believe yours will be, too!

Your brother-in-grace,
*Pastor Jack Hayford*
*Chancellor and Founder*
*The King's University*
*Los Angeles, California*

# Introduction

I wrote the following words in my journal twenty years ago:

*Does anyone else get tangle-brain trying to understand how Grace and the Law fit together? I know we are saved by grace—not by our works. Since heaven doesn't have a citizenship lottery, my only hope was for a free pass. Jesus provided one for me.[1] I feel forgiven and know I'm going to be in heaven forever. What puzzles me is how "Be forgiven" works with "Be good." The problem is I keep sinning. I get tempted, and often the temptation gets me (if you know what I mean)! I know Jesus is my Advocate-Atoner, the One who takes away my sin, so I confess. I receive forgiveness and cleansing from those stains on my soul.[2] Right?*

Do those words echo your thoughts? If so, this book is for you! I continued writing . . .

*Where does all the condemnation come from? When I violate His commands, such overwhelming shame and guilt press in on me, that I can hardly bear to talk to the One who assures my ultimate forgiveness. That doesn't make any sense. If He only hates the sin—not the sinner (me)—why am I so reluctant to come into His presence after I have done wrong? If I am no longer "under law, but under grace,"[3] why is the Law's voice still so loud judging me? Does God want me to feel disgusted with myself? Because I . . .*

How does "Be good" fit together with "Be forgiven"? That is an unsettling question that gnaws at our soul and spills into our mind, again and again, accompanied by other anxious speculations: *Can things ever be the same between God and me after what I've done? Am I still saved? Have I fallen away?*

And as the cover of this book intimates: *Can I truly settle the guilt that unsettles me?*

We know we're supposed to confess our sins after our guilty actions—and receive forgiveness. But many times, the guilt doesn't go away. Especially after we have flagrantly violated God's will or way, the guilt stares us in the face. Even if we secretly enjoy the sin and have no idea how to resist it, we truly want the temptation gone!

The more we truly want to do right—and fail—the heavier our guilt feels. It grows far beyond a time-specific reality and becomes a dark atmosphere under which we live. Self-condemnation and self-reproach oppress us with unbearable weight. Our wrongdoing feels, somehow, like a special case of failure. We find it nearly impossible to forgive ourselves, and we are haunted by the evil we allowed in our lives.

Why do we have such a wrestling match with truth? Why is it so difficult to accept the forgiveness we know Jesus offers to us? Why does regret about our past sometimes steal away hope for our future? And why do we end up not just hating what we did, but hating our very selves for doing it?

Most Christians (or, as I refer to them, followers or believers) just assume that those guilt feelings and threats about eternity come from God. But do they?

Ask yourself—as I asked myself—does the argument against God's long-suffering mercy ring true with the other things you know and experience from Him? Is the voice of severe condemnation you hear really the voice of the God of love? Is the conversation in your mind just between you and God? Or, is there another voice—similar-sounding in many ways to yours or God's, but not exactly the same? The voice we hear may not be our own—or God's.

What do I mean by that?

Consider the overall difference between Jesus, our Shepherd, and the devil, our accuser. Jesus is a burden-bearer who takes our anxiety away.

By contrast, our adversary "prowls around"[4] like a savage beast looking to devour us. Do your questions, feelings, and worries about the Law bring you peace—or make you fretful? Do they build you up—or eat you up inside?

Who threatens the sheep—the shepherd or the wolf?

When we can't explain the anxious feelings of dread, guilt, or self-reproach, there may be far more going on than just a discussion with ourselves. Might there be a sinister presence, an insubstantial but very real entity in our minds, whispering falsehoods and challenging the truth of God's word?

I believe, sometimes, there is.

---

[1]  Ephesians 2:1-9
[2]  1 John 1:8-10
[3]  Romans 6:14
[4]  1 Peter 5:7-8

# Chapter 1

# Spirit of the Pharisee

---

Life in Jesus is not always easy.

Even leaving aside the difficulties of avoiding temptation, maturing in our walk, and making disciples like Jesus asked us to do, just getting an accurate picture of what God is like is tough. I'm fond of telling people who have rejected Jesus' love, "I don't believe in the God you don't believe in." Frequently in conversations, even with fellow followers of Christ, I find myself thinking, *God is not like that.*

Many of my friends have distorted views about God—His motives, His priorities, and His ways. Frankly, God seems to get a bum rap far more often than He gets thanks!

God tells us that the three human sentiments most closely associated with His intention for us are faith, hope and love.[1] One of the simplest ways to tell if something comes from Him—stuff that happens or things we hear in our minds—is to ask ourselves, *Do I have more hope for the future? Do I want to entrust myself even more into His hands? Can I feel His love?*

**The truth is that everything He arranges in life is wrapped in mercy.**

He is good and filled with such love that He perpetually does good for each of us. The truth is that everything He arranges in life is wrapped in mercy.[2]

He is kind. He fixes. He forgives. He makes a way when there is no way forward.

Not everyone—or everything—tells you the truth about what God is like.

## The Evil-Spirited

Though we do not talk about it all the time, believers engage in almost constant warfare with spiritual terrorists who infiltrate our thoughts and emotions to sabotage the conclusions we draw about God, others, and ourselves. The wrestling match goes on inside our minds and throughout "heavenly places."[3] Out-in-the-open pitched battles against our opponents are few; skirmishes with the hidden ones are many.

**The unseen world is more real than what we behold on this planet with our eyes.**

Though western and scientific culture scoff at the existence of a spiritual dimension beyond the limits of physical measurement and observation, we know exactly the opposite: this tangible world only exists because it was formed out of the spiritual realm,[4] and the unseen world is more real than what we behold on this planet with our eyes.[5]

Jesus Himself was confronted by satanic temptation,[6] so it seems foolish to imagine that we won't be. In fact, one of the primary proofs He offered about His kingdom authority was casting out evil spirits, and healing all who were "oppressed" by demonic presences.[7] The evil-spirited are exactly that—beings whose entire identities and assignments are against God's marvelous ways and truth. These forces are spiritual, not natural to our flesh-and-blood world. Consequently, while practice can help us spot their brand of evil,[8] discerning their presence, as well as their identity, often requires some spiritual gifting.[9] They are not-so-easily-identifiable.

Manifestations of these featureless powers may be as straightforward and occasional as a temptation, or as complicated to explain as a poor self-image.

Evil-spirited beings can cause sickness, fractured relationships, nightmares, or disturbances to the mind. All too easily, they break into the inner parts of our minds with negative (and repeated) thoughts about our future or ourselves. They say things like, *"You are so stupid—I can't believe the way you always mess things up!"* Or, *"God doesn't care about you."*

Interestingly, we rarely think to trace those heavily laden thoughts back to their true source. Because the voices sound like our own, we do not challenge their legit-

**Because the voices sound like our own, we do not challenge their legitimacy.**

imacy. It's hard to distinguish between our normal thinking and their spiritual tinkering. We fall prey to foreign thought patterns that protest everything God desires for us, especially His mercy and affection.

The exact thoughts are hard to pin down—and even harder to silence. Like school children practicing for a play, we repeat the lines prompted by these off-stage callers. The lines we're fed blanket us in feelings of depression, self-rejection, and disapproval. They wrap us in despair or unbelief, and easily confuse us about our destiny or identity.

They are not spooky-scary evil from a Hollywood movie set; they are like weed-seeds of ruin, grief, adversity, barrenness, and disappointment wanting to plant themselves everywhere. Much of the Church says nothing about them, and many sincere believers are skeptical that anything so intangible could make such a mess of things in our lives. Other segments of the Church exaggerate the power and presence of the evil-spirited, and attribute too much of what goes on in and around us to them.

We don't really know what to call them. Our naming tools are clumsy and approximate because, as I've said, these forces rarely show themselves openly. Their greatest weapon is the obscurity that allows them to plant false thoughts and feelings in our mind—without us realizing what has been done to us. We might not know their name, but sometimes we spot their game. Occasionally, they make a frontal assault against us and manifest so obviously that there is no mistaking their presence.

I had a sudden encounter with such a fleshless foe.

## Accosted in Athens

In 2009, George Patsaouras, the national leader of the Foursquare denomination in Greece, invited me to teach a series on "*The Law and Grace*." He wanted me to explain how believers in Christ are supposed to relate to the Law of Moses, and why so many of us continue to battle with guilt and condemnation. It's not an easy subject because many verses in the Bible seem to be at odds with one another.

Though I had never made a thorough verse-by-verse study on the subject, I agreed to do the three-evening seminar months before the event. As the teaching opportunity approached, I was excited to share what I had discovered—simple truths that radically changed my own thinking about guilty feelings, fears of losing my salvation, and the nature of true righteousness.

My travel itinerary before arriving in Athens involved a three-week teaching tour that included Australia, Singapore, Korea, and Thailand. After leaving Southeast Asia, I had a stopover in India for 36 hours—just long enough to take advantage of my around-the-world airline ticket. Such airfares have one cost regardless of layovers, so I stopped to take a pastor-couple to dinner in Bangalore.

Flying from India to Greece was going to be a stretch. Knowing an eventual reality, however, isn't quite the same as experiencing it. For a guy who generally goes to bed before 9:30pm, I was already a bit out of my element by 11:00pm when I flew from Bangalore to Mumbai. My eyes glazed over even further in Mumbai between landing, changing terminals at 1:00am, and boarding my onward flight to London at 2:00am. The plane touched down in London 13 hours later—just in time for me to miss, by ten minutes, my backtracking connection to Greece. I managed to endure three hours in the hectic and crowded Heathrow terminal before boarding for the remaining leg of my air-marathon, the four-hour flight to Athens.

Passing through immigration and customs, I finally emerged from Eleftherios Venizelos (Athens) Airport exactly one hour before the seminar was to begin—but it is a fifty-minute drive to get to the church.

On the wild ride there, Pastor George explained why he wanted me to speak about Christians and the Law: "The Greek culture is steeped in religious thinking. When people make a commitment to Christ, they have a difficult time putting off their religious and legalistic mindset. This is a problem, and it prevents them from truly maturing in Christ."

Funny, his explanation of the Greeks sounded suspiciously suitable for many believers, including myself!

Pastor George's congregation, the largest evangelical church in Greece, is actually five-in-one. The main services and training events like this one are translated simultaneously into Bulgarian, Polish, Romanian, and Spanish. The newly built sanctuary accommodates this unusual linguistic challenge. The second-floor balcony seats almost as many people as the auditorium itself, and each seat has its own set of earphones for listening to the message in their own language. The translators sit in one of four specially designed booths inset in the back wall.


## An "Angel of Light"

When the car pulled up to the church, I heard music and realized just how close we were to the start of the service. I quickly opened the back-seat car door, grabbed my backpack (and my suitcase) to head into the church. Getting myself into the right frame of mind to begin the teaching was a bit challenging. Trying to shrug off the effects of intercontinental air travel, I took one, two deep breaths and mentally whispered a quick, "Thank You, Lord."

As soon as I emerged from the car, a man with a heavy German accent asked me, "Are you Dr. Daniel Brown?"

Mindful of my jetlagged condition, I paused several seconds before responding, "Yes, I am." (I confess that I wanted to check my passport just to be certain.) Almost immediately, however, I thought to myself, *How do you know I am Daniel Brown?* For the briefest moment, I admit I had the very unchristian thought, *paparazzi?* But no camera shutters began clicking.

He then inquired, "Are you going to teach the people about what's to come—in the future?"

Not completely confident of my answer in my sleep-deprived condition, I did an internal double-check before replying, "I don't think so. This is not a seminar about end times. I am teaching about grace. This is a seminar on the grace of God."

I thought he might have been confused by what someone might have told him about the event. *How widely did they publicize this seminar?* I wondered.

Without hesitating, without even responding to what I said, he fired back, "But will you teach them about what is to come?"

I realized, then, he was not confused. He had an agenda! My mind was instantly flooded with a Bible passage:

> We fight not against flesh and blood, but against the rulers, against the powers, against the world forces of this darkness, against the spiritual forces of wickedness in the heavenly places.

The verse from Ephesians 6:12 came unbidden to my thoughts, and the abrupt oddness in the atmosphere told me, with some certainty, I was confronting a man tormented by an evil spirit.

## An Ancient Heresy

Remembering that we are limited by clumsy and approximate language to name the evil-spirited, I'm going to call the thought-manipulating foe I faced the *Spirit of the Pharisee*. I give it that name because the Pharisees were a group of Jewish leaders who strictly abided by the Law of Moses. Though they believed in adhering meticulously to the letter of the Law, they almost always ignored the spirit of the Law—the reason the Law was given in the first place.

Jesus reserved His harshest condemnations for the Pharisees, whose legalistic religion had strayed far from God's intent and purpose. The

Pharisees expected Jesus to agree with their low opinion of sinners and their high opinion of their own spirituality. Instead, He shocked (and upset) them by drawing close to people whose sinful conditions set them well below the Pharisees' acceptable standards of righteousness.

**Jesus reserved His harshest condemnations for the Pharisees.**

In general, people in the church world refer to the mentality of those long-ago teachers of the Law as *legalism*. I will define *legalism* over and over throughout this book because a single, simple definition cannot capture all of its nuances and the many ways it influences our thinking. As we will see, it produces large quantities of self-righteousness, judgment, and condemnation.

*Legalism* majors in guilt and misguided sacrifice—urging its followers to evaluate their relationship with God on the basis of standards and scores for their performance, rather than on the basis of love and faith. *Legalism* condemns people for their deeds-in-the-flesh, rather than celebrating God for His work-on-the-Cross. It points out our insufficiency, instead of God's all-sufficiency.

*Legalism* was a huge problem in the early church. Teachers of this heresy were "disturbing" and "troubling" Christ's Church in its earliest days.[10] Barely 500 miles from where I stood confronting this ancient spirit, "false brethren" tried to "secretly" "spy out [the] liberty" among Galatian believers 2,000 years ago.[11] Paul stood up to those false teachers. He refused to "yield in subjection to them for even an hour, so that the truth of the gospel" would not be snatched from believers' hearts.[12] He spoke out forcefully against the *Spirit of the Pharisee,* and its false prophets—no matter how spiritually correct they appeared:

> But even if we, or an angel from heaven, should preach to you a gospel
> contrary to what we have preached to you, he is to be accursed [anathema]!
> —Galatians 1:8

7

Paul grew alarmed because his spiritual children were tempted by legalists to return to the provisions of the Law. He wanted to know who had "bewitched" them with false representations.[13] Why would they "turn back again to the weak and worthless elemental" things of the Law?[14] Grace plus "works of the Law" was "a different gospel" than what Paul preached.[15]

## Doctrines of Demons

A false gospel, however religious it appears, is an evil message! The true nature of evil has almost nothing to do with beings and powers suggested by Hollywood. The forces of evil are not empowered by energies that call for special effects and a movie camera. Mostly, the evil-spirited are as featureless as a virus or some bacterium. What makes them evil is their determination to push people away from God's desire for them.

The Bible refers to demonically inspired ideas and religious systems as "doctrines of demons."[16] The deceitful "religions" taught by evil spirits warp God's truth in order to lead people away from the tenderness of His heart toward them, and the greatness of His plans for them. False gods, evil-spirited beings offer "teachings" (though completely counterfeit) in the same way that the true God does. God teaches us how to live and how to profit;[17] false gods try to mislead us into loss, death, and destruction.[18] Evil beings and evil impulses distort the truth of the True God—becoming false focal points (idols) of worship.[19] Unknowingly, we sometimes subscribe to their teachings and unwittingly serve them rather than Him.

> **The deceitful "religions" taught by evil spirits warp God's truth in order to lead people away from the tenderness of His Heart.**

The teachings of *legalism* subtly disrupt our love-relationship with Jesus. By concentrating on our shortcomings, *legalism* robs us of the joyful intimacy God wants us to have with Him. It steals away what should be an unshakeable assurance of our sin-proof relationship with God. Literally, it corrupts and perverts the good news of Jesus.

The man I encountered on the steps of pastor George's church was manipulated by an evil-spirited foe, and he was propagating that false god's catechism. He was a zealous evangelist for a god-who-is-no-god.[20] Heedless of my answers, and Pastor George's attempts to move him away (so I could get into the church to start teaching), the prophet of *legalism* grew increasingly adamant in his demand: "You must teach the people about the judgment of God!"

He was overwhelmed by the *Spirit of the Pharisee* and almost couldn't help but blurt out the religious wrongness inspired by his cruel taskmaster. So, just as Jesus once rebuked Peter,[21] I spoke directly into his confusion: "No, I don't! I will teach them about the great and loving grace of God."

With a look of rage and disgust, he pointed at the sanctuary I was attempting to reach and exclaimed, "But there is sin in this church!"

## Really?!

I should pause a moment for yet another confession. Having pastored people for nearly 35 years, I am a trained professional; I don't necessarily disclose all my thoughts with my words or facial expressions. I can have two thoughts at the same time—and one of those thoughts usually finds the humor in such situations. "*No kidding,*" I wanted to reply. "*Sin in this church? Let me guess—there are probably people in there, too?!*"

I was torn between smiling and frowning at the absurdity of what the tormented man said. He got a revelation about sin in a church in Greece and traveled all the

**No one needs a revelation to discover sin in church.**

9

way from Northern Europe to make his point?! That's laughable! No one needs a revelation to discover sin in church. It takes a bit more revelation to spot the sin in our own life,[22] but that is another subject. He could have stayed in his own country and randomly picked any church to scold.

Raising his voice in a spiritual menace, as though he expected his curse to open the earth beneath my feet, he cried out, "You are a servant of the Enemy. You are teaching about grace to a church full of sin. God is bringing His judgment against the Church [in Athens]!"

**He speaks to us of deliverence and salvation—not of wrath!**

*How interesting,* I thought. *I have been invited to teach about the grace of God, and the very spirit of legalism that has been browbeating these saints tried to intercept me and hijack the Gospel with threats of judgment.* Strangely but wonderfully emboldened to "fight the good fight of faith,"[23] I responded to his threat with one of my favorite questions: "Have you read the Book?"

If he had read the whole Bible, he would know that:

- God promises never to be angry with His people again.[24]
- Anyone who believes in His Son has "passed out of judgment."[25]
- Those who have "been justified by His blood," are "saved from the wrath of God" through Christ.[26]

I don't often raise my voice, but this situation seemed to call for a bit more punctuation than normal. I loudly inquired, "Why would I be talking to daughters and sons of the Most High about the anger and judgment of God? He speaks to us of deliverance and salvation—not of wrath!"


**Conflicting Realities**

Actually, though, the guy had a point—not the one Jesus wants to press foremost into our hearts, but an undeniable point, nonetheless: We do have sin in our lives! Even doing our best to follow Jesus, we live with two realities that are difficult to reconcile with one another. On the one hand, we believe we are saved, forgiven, and going to Heaven; but on the other hand, we are sinful, failing—and worried we aren't going to Heaven. Honest followers of Christ are only too mindful of falling "short of the glory of God."[27]

The ongoing wrongness in our lives produces deep condemnation and worrisome anxiety that we may have crossed some invisible line, taxing God's grace beyond its limits. So, how do we balance the undeniable existence of sin (Law-breaking) in our lives, and the equally clear promise of forgiveness? Sincere believers-in-Jesus continue to sin after receiving grace and forgiveness. We cannot deny our waywardness in matters great and small! We want to do good, and know we are supposed to think and behave righteously; nevertheless, we make poor choices many times a day.

Trying hard. Losing big. Which voiced verdict are we supposed to believe—the Law that shouts, "Guilty and condemned!" or Grace that whispers, "Forgiven and justified"? The voice of the Law seems much louder than the voice of Grace. Accusations usually outweigh assurances.

**Accusations usually outweigh assurances.**

How the Law of God and the Grace of God overlap and fit together is a complicated concept to grasp. God gave both of them as expressions of His love for us—even though they came at different times and through different spokespeople. As the Scriptures say, "the Law was given through Moses; grace and truth were realized through Jesus Christ."[28]

And that may be the first point of encouragement for you in your own walk with Christ. If you toss back and forth in your mind; if you have questions—and worries; if you struggle with condemnation, you are normal. Even Jesus grew in wisdom over the course of His life,[29] so it stands to reason that you and I still have things to learn in the Kingdom. The Bible encourages us to ask God for wisdom, knowing that He grants us understanding without scolding us and telling us we should have already figured things out by now![30]

## Honest Questions

Because we love God, we truly want to live the way He wants us to live. Despite lapses and even seasons of rebellion when we aren't quite willing or able to abandon a sin He has fingered in our life, we do want to do His will. We want to obey His commands and make right choices.

Most of the time.

May I make a confession? Sometimes, I don't; often I fail. That's when the torture sets in—and when worry eats at my soul.

When we knowingly walk off the path into sin's wasteland; when we allow bitterness to take root; when we crave what isn't ours; when we lie, cheat or steal; when we take *that* drink or flip through *that* magazine or fantasize about *that* scenario; when we do wrong, what then? What do we do? What does God do?

That's what this book is about. When does *relying* on grace become *presuming* on grace? If I go—sincerely intending to sin no more—but then sin again, will Jesus stand from kneeling and grab a stone in His hand?

For decades I realized that there was something inadequate in my understanding about the Law and Grace—about guilt and forgiveness. I simply couldn't find a permanent place to land in my thinking, and too often my doctrine seemed at odds with my feelings. This book is my story—not just a travel-log of a few summer days in Greece, but a catalog of the many changes God brought to my thinking while preparing for the lecture in Athens, and while being there.

It will take awhile for you to read, but nowhere near as long as it took me to realize how to be completely mindful of my sin, without worrying about my intimate relationship with Jesus. I hope to tell you what God is really like even when you behave so out of character with the person He is transforming you into.

---

[1] 1 Corinthians 13:13
[2] Psalm 145:9
[3] Ephesians 6:12
[4] Hebrews 11:3; Psalm 33:6
[5] 2 Corinthians 4:18
[6] Matthew 4:1-11
[7] Acts 10:38
[8] Hebrews 5:14
[9] 1 Corinthians 12:10
[10] Galatians 1:7; 5:12
[11] Galatians 2:4
[12] Galatians 2:5
[13] Galatians 3:1, 3
[14] Galatians 4:9
[15] 2 Corinthians 11:4
[16] 1 Timothy 4:1
[17] Isaiah 44:10; 48:17
[18] John 10:10
[19] Deuteronomy 11:16; Psalm 106:36; Luke 16:13; 1 Thessalonians 1:9
[20] Galatians 4:8
[21] Mark 8:32-33
[22] Matthew 7:1-5
[23] 1 Timothy 6:12; 2 Timothy 4:7
[24] Isaiah 54:9-10
[25] John 3:16-19; 5:24
[26] Romans 5:9
[27] Romans 3:23
[28] John 1:17
[29] Luke 2:52
[30] James 1:5

# Chapter 2

# Legalism and the Trap

---

The fierce man who accosted me that evening in Greece was confused and animated by an evil-spirited distortion masquerading as spiritual orthodoxy. In short, he was a heretic. Perhaps his uncertainty about the finished work Jesus did on the Cross left him prey to religious-sounding lies. His distortions, though extreme, reminded me just how confusing it can be to navigate between the Law and Grace—and why the Church struggles to find the balance between *legalism* and *license*.

What are we supposed to make of the guilty feelings that plague us? Why, if we are forgiven, do those doubts and accusations persist? Why do we labor with such pangs of conscience that turn into self-condemnation? Why do we think we should keep our distance from God for a few days after we sin horribly?

**Why do we think we should keep our distance from God for a few days after we sin horribly?**

Let's begin by acknowledging that the whole issue is confusing. Grace isn't a simple subject to neatly package. On the one hand, some teachers profess that sin no longer matters at all because God's love and grace magically eliminates it as a factor in our lives. According to their narrow reading of the Bible, God is [only] love, and love only acts lovingly; consequently, God would never do anything to inflict pain or punishment on those He loves (i.e. everyone). They suggest that we needn't pay attention to our consciousness of sin; whether we're guilty or not isn't important because God is going to issue a blanket-pardon to everyone.

The heresy is subtle, but they want us to disbelieve the reality of hell—and any unpleasant consequences in eternity.

Equally off-center are other instructors who focus so intently on "sin in the camp" that they leave everyone feeling totally inadequate and unqualified for Grace. To them, God may be loving, and He has, indeed, forgiven people; however, those people (you and I) should live relatively sinless lives thereafter. They imply that God is a reluctant Savior who, because of covenant stipulations, is required to forgive and save, but He's not very happy about it. Give Him an excuse to cut people out of Grace, and He will gladly take it. Though they might not say it quite so plainly, these teachers hint that each sin we commit brings us closer to "the eternal chopping-block."

Both these notions are imbalanced, and they leave us feeling as though we have but two choices: (1) Simply ignore the guilt we feel, and think of our sins as a persistent nuisance in our spiritual lives, or (2) Scramble to work our way back into God's good graces—until we no longer feel guilty.

## Confusing Questions

Generally speaking, Christians grow impatient with matters that force them to think systematically about their faith. They much prefer quick, single-sentence solutions to their spiritual quandaries. Sometimes, though, we arrive at simple understandings only after *less-than-simple* explanations.

You should find comfort knowing that questions about guilt, condemnation and relationship with God came up in the early Church, centuries before you began wrestling with them. Some non-believing Jews accused Paul of persuading "men to worship God contrary to the law."[1] Other believing Jews wondered if faith nullified the Law.[2] Perhaps the most telling question found in the New Testament, at least as it relates to the confusion about how Law and Grace work together in our lives, is found in Paul's letter to the Galatians. He tries to shake their thinking by asking, "Is the Law then contrary to the promises of God?"[3]

15

He answers with a resounding, "May it never be."

But for much of my Christian life, my sincere answer to his question would have been, I *don't think so, but I'm not really clear on the details.* If I had encountered the Athens prophet of judgment a few years earlier, he might have been able to win me over—or at least confuse me with his twisted but sincere beliefs about "sin in the church" and what God wanted done about that sin.

**Is my sin ever too gross for God's forgiveness?**

We who are led by the Spirit of God are no longer "under the Law";[4] and Paul declared, "Christ is the end of the law for righteousness to everyone who believes."[5] Yet how do we understand those verses in light of Jesus saying He came to fulfill, not "abolish the Law"?[6] The angry man in Athens seemed to have such certain answers for the questions most of us struggle to solve:

- Is the Law still in effect? What happens when I break the Law?
- If I have been good for a long, long time, then blow it, does any of my "good" count against my "bad"?
- How many times will God believe and accept my repentance for a habitual sin?
- Is my sin ever too gross for God's forgiveness?

## Legalism

Even if you have never heard the railings of an angry crusader from northern Europe, you have heard the merciless and disapproving tone of the *Spirit of the Pharisee* in your own mind. It wears a religious mask. Its mistruths sound holy, profound, and right. But they are not. Buried beneath the religious exterior of its heresies, you will always discover condemnation and a terrible burden. *Legalism* tells us we have fallen short. We have disappointed God. We must try harder and be better. Hope is running out; grace has nearly come to an end of its limits.

Much like long-ago civilizations believed that the earth was flat, and people who sailed to the edge of the world would fall off, some believers imagine that God's grace has ends from which people can fall. That is not what the New Testament teaches. It is the teaching of the *Spirit of the Pharisee*; it is the basis of *legalism* whose four tenets follow one from the other:

1. There is a limit to the number or the nature of sins covered by God's grace;
2. By sinning too frequently or too grossly, you will transgress beyond the edge of its covering (likely, you already have);
3. Once your sins exceed the allotted measure of God's grace, you "fall from grace."
4. If you want to avoid "falling from grace," you must be more obedient and offer more sacrifice to God.

**Infinite Grace**

None of those statements are true, but they sound religiously correct. Like an evil ventriloquist imitating God, *legalism* leaves us feeling scolded, rejected, and condemned. Pause for a moment to consider: does that sound like the end-game intent of the Good Shepherd who pursues us with goodness and mercy, who prepares a full table and cup for us—no matter who else might oppose us?[7] Does it make sense for Him to throw a banquet for us in the presence of our enemies just so He can browbeat us? The whole of Scripture testifies that "He is good, for His loving-kindness is everlasting,"[8] so why would He change His bent so suddenly toward you?

> **Like an evil ventriloquist imitating God, legalism leaves us feeling condemned.**

17

The amount of sin has little meaning in the equation of grace. Grace is somewhat like the concept of infinity. You remember learning about infinity in grade school: no matter how you apply other numbers to it with any mathematical function, it remains infinity. Multiply it by 1,763 and it's still infinity; subtract 43,865,098 from infinity, and it is still infinity. If infinity is on either side of an equation (i.e. to the left or right of the equal sign), the correct answer is always infinity. No number is significant next to it.

So it is with grace: neither the size nor the frequency of sin changes the answer.

Probably because the Law amplifies our sense of what isn't right in our own lives, we make the mistake of concluding that its only purpose is to make us feel ashamed (and rejected). As we will see, that isn't the way the Holy Spirit uses the Law. It is, however, the terrible message the sin-spotter from Northern Europe tried to claim as a prophetic word from God. Sinful people need rescue, but they do not disgust God. He moves toward them with compassion, not condemnation. He grieves over what sin does to us, but He is not mad at us. That is what God is like.

The primary reason the Pharisees rejected Jesus as Messiah was because He offered healing, forgiveness, and deliverance to sinners.[9] They were outraged at Jesus' "blasphemy" when He presumed to "forgive sins,"[10] and were appalled that Jesus mixed so comfortably with "sinners."[11]

The Pharisees prized judgment over mercy,[12] and imagined that God's primary goal was to bring deserved judgment to the earth, rather than to do good to Law-breakers. They expected that any messenger from God would congratulate the righteous and condemn the unrighteous. The *Spirit of the Pharisee* wants judgment now! I'll explain why over the course of this book, but as you are just becoming familiar with that false god and its teachings, I mostly want to tell you how merciless and judgmental it

**Jesus came to suspend judgment, not to hurry it along.**

is. *Legalism* presses for a guilty verdict and demands punishment for the guilty. That isn't what God is like; Jesus came to suspend judgment, not to hurry it along.

## Sin in the Church

But how could I argue against such an obvious truth as sin in the church? I see sin in my own life. If others are only partially the sinner I am, any church is engulfed in sin. Religious, legalistic prophets use that reality as a premise for condemnation, whereas God uses it as a beginning point for Grace:

> . . . For all have sinned and fall short of the glory of God, being justified as a gift by His grace through the redemption which is in Christ Jesus . . .
> —Romans 3:23-24

Jesus "gave Himself for our sins so that He might rescue us," not condemn us.[13] Shouting prophets like the one in Athens are very convincing,[14] but they are empowered by a "different spirit" than the Holy Spirit.[15] They use guilt to mount a furious assault against believers-in-Christ. They pronounce judgment against our failures.

Instead of teaching us about the kindness and generosity of God, *legalism* attempts to convince us that He is either unable or unwilling to cover our sins with forgiveness and love. The *Spirit of the Pharisee* commandeers our sincere efforts to be more spiritual—to become "better" Christians. The basic message it communicates goes something like this:

> God's grace saved you and covered your sins up to that point in your life when you accepted Jesus' sacrifice on the Cross. However, God expects you to do (most of) the work from now on. Your status with God depends on your level of obedience. The better you keep His commands, the better He will feel about you and the more He will love you.

19

That spiritual badgering drives us toward an unthinkable conclusion that is the underbelly, the dark side of legalistic teaching; it wants us to believe that Jesus' work on the Cross is insufficient for our whole life. Jesus did His part, but He only did part of the work for our salvation. The rest is up to us.

Such suggestions profoundly unsettle our soul. We know we should be better people, and we understand we should be more righteous. We have no defense against accusations of sin. We are sinners. And so, our souls scramble in dismay like cadets under surprise review, knowing their living quarters are not ready for inspection. *Oh no*, our hearts wail, *If judgment comes today, I know my house is not in order. What can I do?*

*Legalism* uses guilt as a whip, and drives us to live as though what Christ did is not (quite) enough.

**The Trap**

The grossness and continued existence of sin in our life leaves us feeling terribly insecure. Whatever others may think about us, we know within ourselves that we are not good. We are unrighteous. Our sins steal away our confidence to approach God. Especially when we've made a big mistake or done something terribly wrong, "faith alone" seems too flimsy a foundation upon which to stand. Overwhelmed by guilt, we want to stand on something that seems more substantial to remedy our broken connection with God.

> **Legalism uses guilt as a whip, and drives us to live as though what Christ did is not (quite) enough.**

Driven by anxiety and guilt, we try to add our own work to what He did on Calvary. When our guilty shame wears us down, we attempt to tip the scales back in our favor by making promises, swearing vows, doing penance, or otherwise trying to be "better." It isn't as though we doctrinally subscribe to such a false teaching, but subconsciously we remain vulnerable to the lie that says God will continue to favor us only if we are able to maintain a minimal level of goodness.

Believers are not tempted to come back and live under the Law because of its harsh treatment of sin or its demands for sacrifice. Who would want to again be subject to such judgment and condemnation?[16] No, what tempts us back under the Law is our sincere desire to make things right with God. We want to please Him. We want to repair the damage we have done.

Normally, we use a word like temptation to refer to something nasty, immoral, or clearly against God's plan. But the true essence of sin is any way other than God's way. Sometimes even religious-looking notions can be unrighteous.[17] And tempting. The overwhelming temptation to make things right on our own is a terrible trap.

> **The overwhelming temptation to make things right on our own is a terrible trap.**

As a false God, the *Spirit of the Pharisee* lures us back under the Law as the means by which we can secure a more tangible justification. It offers us counterfeit assurance. By falsely linking our acceptance by God to our ability to be "good" (or at least "better"), we wind up living under the Old Covenant after we agreed to the New one.

The deception makes sense to our bewildered soul: "God is holy, so the holier we are, the more God will love us and accept us." The ancient heresy springs the trap:

> With my help, you can rid yourself of sin. If you try very, very hard to live according to the dictates of the Law (especially avoiding the big nasties), you can become good enough to be worthy of relationship with God.
>
> Even if you are not perfectly perfect, concentrate on your guiltiness and make promises to God that you will never, ever do those things again. You are on probation, having used up most of your allotment of grace and

forgiveness. God is watching you—and evaluating His relationship with you based on how well you keep His Law.

## True Righteousness

Does God want us to be righteous? Yes, of course. But on what basis does righteousness become our portion? That is the issue—the point of confusion and consternation for earnest believers like us. We want to be rid of our sin. We grieve over its continued presence in our lives, and we yearn for an ever-more-intimate relationship with God. Our sincerity seeks answers to both the continued wrongness in our life and the ache in our soul for deeper communion with God. That makes us especially vulnerable to the false teachers who roam the streets of Athens—and the corridors of our own minds.

Was there sin in the church I visited in Athens? Yes. Is there sin in your life? Yes. But that reality is not the essence or the entirety of the Gospel of Christ. Sin may abound, but grace abounds "all the more."[18]

The true Gospel boldly declares that God has forgiven us every sin of our entire lives: "For by one offering He has perfected for all time those who are being sanctified."[19]

**Our sin is the beginning point for the good news, not a disqualification from it.**

To whatever extent sin may have reign in a believer's life, it has been supplanted by the stronger, more lasting dominion of grace. Grace now reigns "through righteousness to bring eternal life through Jesus Christ our Lord."[20] According to the true Gospel, sin has been kicked off its throne, and it has no say whatsoever in our forever relationship with God. And, "where there is forgiveness of these things, there is no longer any offering for sin."[21]

Can my sin affect aspects of my life in Christ? Yes, and we will explore all of this in greater detail in the chapters that follow, but our sin is the beginning point for the good news, not a disqualification from it.

## Backwards Message

The angry man who confronted me may have sounded like a Christian who was zealous for righteousness in the Church, but he pointed people toward the wrong path to righteousness. He was like teachers from long ago who plagued the early Church with legalistic prescriptions. They did "not understand either what they [were] saying or the matters about which they [made] confident assertions."[22] Messengers of this false gospel have, through the ages, bid us return to "guilt offerings" and "sin offerings,"[23] the very bondage "from which Christ set us free."[24]

The apostle Paul described the legalistic heretics of his day as zealous and religious—but off-base. Instead of finding in Christ a final and lasting righteousness, they sought a righteousness of their own making. They did not "subject themselves to the righteousness of God."[25]

My encounter with the messenger from the *Spirit of the Pharisee* lasted no more than four or five minutes—just long enough to remind me of religion's stale aftertaste. Who would want such a dour and severe sentinel for their soul? No one; except, perhaps, chosen "prophets" who find fulfillment in being commissioned to condemn the wrong in others' lives.

Pastor George finally stepped bodily in front of the false prophet, who was trying to block my way until he convinced me to pronounce judgment against God's children. He was on a mission of misery, not a mission of mercy. Instead of the dimensionless love of God, he spoke of impending judgment, as though it was the first and most important item on God's agenda.

Actually, judgment is the last thing on God's mind.

Thanks to George's intervention, I was able to proceed inside the sanctuary. I walked quickly, knowing I had but moments before the seminar began. Almost immediately, the atmosphere shifted. The angry insistence and harsh condemnation

**He was on a mission of misery, not a mission of mercy.**

that hung about the man outside like a cloud, evaporated as I stepped quietly into the sanctuary to the final few lines of a worship chorus. I felt like a man holding his breath against poisonous fumes until finally escaping into fresh air. My legs still felt a bit wobbly, but what a relief to draw breath from God's Spirit.


## Sanctuary Seminar

Besides, I was conducting a "seminar" in church. Before I became a full-time pastor, I taught literature and philosophy at various colleges. That is where I picked up a passion to lay out, in coherent fashion, truths and topics of the Kingdom. My two worlds converged on that hot, summer night in Athens. A lecture in church—music to my soul.

After dropping my backpack on a front row chair, I took a few deep breaths, grabbed my Bible and climbed the several steps leading to the platform and the awaiting translator, Angela. Though everyone had come from a long day of work, I counted on the fact that most of my Greek friends struggled with the same question I had for much of my believing life: *"If we are no longer under the Law, what purpose does it serve in my life?"*

I paused for a moment to take in the sight of scores of believers who wanted to hear how they could come out from under the Law. They wanted to know what to do with lingering feelings of guilt. When their own souls condemned them and confirmed that surely, God could not use them in ministry, how should they reply?

Love filled me. It suspended the physical effects of jetlag. Like a broom sweeping up broken pieces of glass, the sudden rush of love in my heart brushed away the rattled feelings from the spiritual gauntlet I had just run. The angry shouts and denunciations outside couldn't find a way into the sanctuary where the love of God created such peace and joy. It was almost like being in a soundproof room. Everything was still—and somehow muted. I interpreted the spiritual hush as a promise from God to me and my fellow travelers. The prattle and pressure coming from the animated prophet outside simply ceased to have any meaning in the presence of Jesus. It was all the confirmation I needed.

Certain that I was where Jesus wanted me to be, I said, "Good evening everyone. I have very, very good news for you: the grace and love of God are 'more than enough' for all our sins."[26] Shouted *amens* rose from amidst the congregation. As the *hallelujahs* faded into the air, I whispered thanks to God for the privilege of being another sort of messenger—one who comforts God's people and "kindly" calls out, "Your 'warfare has ended'; your 'iniquity has been removed'."[27]

---

[1]   Acts 18:13; 21:28
[2]   Romans 3:31
[3]   Galatians 3:21
[4]   Galatians 5:18
[5]   Romans 10:4
[6]   Matthew 5:17
[7]   Psalm 23:5-6
[8]   Psalm 136:1
[9]   Luke 5:30-32
[10]  Luke 5:20-24
[11]  See Matthew 9:10-13
[12]  James 2:13
[13]  Galatians 1:3-4
[14]  1 Timothy 1:7
[15]  2 Corinthians 11:4
[16]  Galatians 5:1
[17]  Romans 10:3
[18]  Romans 5:20
[19]  Hebrews 10:14
[20]  Romans 5:21
[21]  Hebrews 10:18
[22]  1 Timothy 1:7
[23]  Leviticus 7:7
[24]  Galatians 5:1
[25]  Romans 10:3-4
[26]  1 Timothy 1:14
[27]  Isaiah 40:1-2

# Chapter 3

# A Force and a Flood

As Angela, my translator, and I adjusted our mics for a quick sound-check, my mind drifted back to the spiritual encounter I just had in the parking lot. I realized that the *Spirit of the Pharisee* had sought inroads to my life several times before. I do not know if that meant I was especially vulnerable to its lies, or if God had been exposing me to it a little at a time over the years, almost like a process of inoculation against a snake's poison.

I remembered a man who named himself "Holy Hubert" at UCLA more than thirty years ago. He spoke—yelled actually—condemnation against hippies, students, communists, fornicators (and anyone else he could think of), while carrying a huge cross hoisted to a leather pouch attached to his belt. *Turn or Burn* was sloppily emblazoned on a banner stringing down from the cross. I imagine he was trying to reach students with his message, but I could not imagine anyone taking him seriously. He was so severe and loveless that he became a mere caricature, a cartoon without humor. His tone, expressions, and ferocity reminded me not at all of the Jesus who whispered in my heart.

During my university days, I, too, was motivated to reach other students by a simple realization: *Oh my gosh, these students will perish if they do not learn of Jesus' sacrifice.* I posted questions and scriptures on the community mirror in our dorm, and I did lots of one-on-one evangelism. I led some outreach discussions and several Bible studies. So, I was no stranger to ministry, and neither was I ashamed of God's good news for my fellow students. But "Holy Hubert" bothered me. I was offended in my spirit. I felt knocked over by him and his angry denunciations of campus sin, not because I felt convicted, but because he was a spiritual imposter.

He tried to manhandle the Gospel's power, arming it for condemnation, not salvation.[1] Hubert's sacrilege struck my spirit like a slap to the face. What draped from his makeshift cross bore no resemblance to what hung from Calvary's. On that rocky outcropping ages ago, God draped the broken body of His Son, on which He etched a forever message: *Be Forgiven*.

> **"Turn or Burn" is worlds apart from "Be Forgiven."**

"Turn or Burn" is worlds apart from "Be Forgiven." Both offer a new future, but an angry, hateful spirit inspires one, while the other, whispered by the Holy Spirit, comes from the very heart of God. What normal person, upon hearing "Holy Hubert's" condemning rants, would eagerly abandon everything in their life just to learn more and follow Hubert's counsel? When people listened to Jesus, they wanted to follow Him and call Him teacher.

I cannot imagine anyone feeling joy from Herbert's message. Nor do you and I feel any joy when we hear those internal voices of condemnation, guiltiness, and disqualification. And yet, Jesus told a parable about a man who felt such joy when he discovered a "treasure hidden in the field," he sold everything he had to buy the entire field.[2] Jesus never changes, correct? While on earth, He attracted sinners like the woman at the well, and He refused to throw the stones religious leaders offered Him. Why then would we imagine that He has changed, now seated at His Father's right hand?

### Spectacle in the Sky

It's sometimes difficult to distinguish "between the holy and the profane,"[3] because wicked things often masquerade as angels of light, and "false apostles" can disguise "themselves as apostles of Christ."[4] However, if you listen closely to the accounts they give you about God, you will more easily tell truth from error.

False gods and their messengers tell a different tale than the One true God. Our God is a God of love who Himself did the necessary work to redeem us from our slavery to sin. He didn't stand back and say, "Measure up." No, He said, "I'll pay the price for you." He is the God of Grace who does for us what we cannot do for ourselves. The Holy Spirit invites us to accept God's provision for "escapes from death."[5]

The *Spirit of the Pharisee* laced Hubert's cross with condemnation like a conspirator sprinkling poison in a drink. What an imposter. Whereas Jesus died for students (and hippies), Hubert only cried against them. Jesus identified with people's sin;[6] Hubert did nothing but point it out. Jesus took our sins upon Himself,[7] and bled out as Advocate. Hubert just yelled out as Accuser. What counterfeit religion. What degradation to drag the Cross into such mean-spirited, pharisaical territory.

The *Spirit of the Pharisee* distorts God's message, transforming it into bad news, instead of good. Inspired by that unkind spirit, men and women with angry and condemning tones parade themselves in church like Hubert did on campus—and call themselves "holy." Such haughty and loveless holiness is actually self-righteousness. Because of their unchallenged claim to holiness, believers and unbelievers alike suppose that God looks down His nose in disgust at failed humanity. They portray Him as angry and condemning, instead of loving and merciful.

The world before, during, and after Jesus' day was like the world today. Our ancestors, our contemporaries, and we ourselves are one (infected) race: sinners one, sinners all. In the midst of rigged justice, bloodlust mockery, petty gambling, violence, and brutality, God chose to lift and suspend His Son as a spectacle-in-the-sky. The Righteous God hung His Son—not "to judge the world, but that the world might be saved through Him."[8]

The Holy-Spirited God, the true God, used the Cross to rescue us from condemnation, not to threaten us with judgment. God's "kind intention" has always been to adopt us as His own, and to "lavish" grace and love upon us.[9] If you do not hear love and grace when God speaks to your spirit—even about your sin—then what you hear is a false spirit.

In my many years pastoring, I encountered numerous individuals who felt as though they could not hear God— yet when condemnation and heavy feelings of guiltiness pressed their souls to loathe themselves and fear for their eternity, they rarely questioned why they suddenly heard Him.

They did not hear the "Good Shepherd"; they heard, instead, the howl of wolves.

> **If you do not hear love and grace when God speaks to your spirit, then what you hear is a false spirit.**

"Holy Hubert" and the false prophet in Greece did not understand God's history with His people. Like many religious-but-misguided people, they snatched isolated glimpses of Old Testament prophets, and tried to act the part. But they did not read the entire script. They missed, completely, the beginning and the end—and the whole point of what God said and did. God's primary longing is not to denounce His people and condemn their sin. He wants to deliver His people and forgive sin. God's overriding passion is to restore our lost relationship with Him.

## The Sin-Force

To set the backdrop for our evenings together, I told the waiting audience we would start with a brief survey of the early Old Testament timeline. I was not surprised to see dismay flicker briefly on some faces. Though I have enjoyed a long relationship with Pastor George's congregation, forged over a dozen years, I doubt many church members would have attended the seminar if they knew they were in for a history lesson. I joked with them about their response, and asked that they give me the evening to change their minds about history—at least, the history of the Bible.

To help you understand why you still feel guilty even though you have been forgiven, I must take you on a journey through parts of the Old

Testament. It does us no good in our search for how we are to relate to the Law and to Grace, if we confine our reading to the New Testament. It is like trying to complete a jigsaw puzzle without the edge pieces.

Unfortunately, many believers find the Old Testament too long to read thoroughly. They tend to read it in small segments, considering only tiny portions at a time. That leads them to several misconceptions about the nature of God and the basis upon which He relates to His people. It's like trying to see a wall-sized mural through a hand-held magnifying glass. Partial reading and incomplete study leave us vulnerable to the very kind of half-quotes and misquotes that fueled confusion in the mind of the angry gentleman outside in the still-hot evening air of Athens.

## A Long Stretch of Time

One of the biggest items we miss by reading the Old Testament piecemeal is the immense period of time it covers. For instance, over 2500 years pass between Adam and Eve in the Garden, and Moses in the desert. Twenty-five centuries zip by in a few nights while reading Genesis. Because we tend to lump together all the events of the Old Testament, we don't realize one of the most startling details of God's history with our race. During the huge span of time from Eden to the Flood, God issued almost no commandments.

> **During that huge span of time, from Eden to the Flood, God issued almost no commandments.**

In addition to "Be fruitful and multiply," God commanded Adam and Eve not to eat from "the tree of the knowledge of good and evil."[10] Because we have heard the story so many times, it is easy to miss the most obvious feature of God's first charge to humanity. It was a single injunction, not a long list of rights and wrongs. One sentence, not even ten commandments. Why was it so uncomplicated, so basic? Why did God not give the first of our kind more rules or warnings or hints for morality?

These simple questions are not easy to answer because so much has changed in our world. Things back then—in the beginning—are difficult to envision today. That is where history comes in. Our forbearers did not need an extensive moral code because, at that point in history, they had no concept of wrong thoughts or behaviors. "*Evil*" was not yet in the world—except for the Serpent. Nothing wicked or immoral suggested itself to Adam and Eve, not even a whisper of thought about things nasty or bratty.

Completely naïve to evil, they were like toddlers in a bathtub. They had no real awareness of their nakedness. It was not until *after* Adam and Eve ate of the fruit that they realized they were undressed[11]—and what such a state might suggest to teenagers a few years after puberty, or to men looking in magazines or on the web.

In the beginning, prior to eating the forbidden fruit, our race knew no evil.[12]

**Infection**

That innocence soon disappeared. Adam and Eve did precisely what we would have done: they violated the one and only command God gave them. Eve first, and Adam soon after, ate the forbidden fruit. Cosmos-altering consequences followed Adam and Eve's violation. Nothing has been the same since because a power called *Sin* invaded the Earth and began its reign over our planet.

When I say sin, I don't mean sin the way you think of sin today. Perhaps *sin-as-a-force* is a more descriptive name for what broke in on our world. Though it may sound like mere semantics, the two types of sin—a spiritual force as opposed to specific acts/thoughts—differ hugely from one another. Without understanding the distinction between the

> **The two types of sin—a spiritual *force* as opposed to specific acts/thoughts—differ hugely from one another.**

*sin-force* that first plagued our race, and the *sin-acts* we carry out today, you miss much of the point of the Law.

The *sin-force* gained access to Eden and began to bend human souls toward evil—like a tractor beam pulling our race in the wrong direction. It wasn't a set of specific thoughts, fantasies, or temptations. Think of the *sin-force* as a deadly infection prior to the appearance of symptoms. Remember the last time you became really sick—as with the flu? Did you know when, exactly, you got sick? You could tell me when the symptoms became undeniable, but not when you caught the bug, right?

The *sin-force* made our ancestors deathly ill, and only later manifested in symptoms—those specific acts and thoughts that today we call "sins." We know coveting and gossiping are sins. It is a sin to steal, lie, or murder. We shouldn't cheat, hold a grudge, or fly off in a rage. Those are sin(s). We generally know when we sin—by crossing a line, by entertaining a thought, or by giving ourselves to something wrong. Even if we quibble about whether or not one of our behaviors is sinful, there is no question in our mind that many other behaviors are definitely sinful.

We can catalog almost any thought or behavior, labeling it sin or not sin.

But in the earliest days of our race, the *sin-force* had few obvious, telltale symptoms. It led people to do wrong before wrong was well defined. Only later did specifically evil activities and thoughts plague our race.[13] God didn't catalog all the symptoms that the unleashed *sin-force* would eventually manifest in humanity's flesh. He simply warned Cain to be on his guard against the *sin-force* because it wanted to overwhelm him. It would take advantage of discouragement, depression—and anytime Cain did not get his own way: "sin is crouching at the door [*of your life*]; and its desire is for you, but you must master it."[14]

The battle was joined between a new foe—the *sin-force*—and humanity. Unquestionably, this newly introduced contaminant would entice and corrupt people. However, God wrote no laws against the specific ways in which the *sin-force* would manifest itself.

Amazing, isn't it, that on the heels of this world-changing development, God instituted no new restraints on human behavior? Even though
vulnerable humans had fallen into the clutches of the *sin-force,* God did
not add substantially to the one command Adam and Eve violated, and
He didn't introduce the Law at that time. He wouldn't do so for almost
2500 years . . .

## The Flood

Sixteen hundred years elapse between the moment the *sin-force* first
infected our race, and the days of Noah. Because the Bible covers those
hundreds of years in merely two chapters, most readers do not catch the
span of time—or its implications. During those centuries, symptoms of
the *sin-force* infection (i.e. *sin-acts*) became
increasingly vile. Instead of the goodness
and righteousness of original Creation,
perversion and evil became the order of the
day. Humanity was corrupted.

**God didn't introduce the Law at that time. He wouldn't do so for almost 2500 years . . .**

Those for whom God made the earth
were ruining it:[15] "The wickedness of man
was great on the earth," and the intent of
their heart was "only evil continually."[16]
Disfigured in heart and mind, humans
introduced unimaginable deformity into God's Creation. God was
"grieved in His heart" and wanted to wash away the filth our muddied
boots had trampled into the cosmos. So, after 1600 years, the Creator
decided to "blot out" all flesh from the face of the earth with a flood of
water.[17]

How many of us have waited even sixteen years for a loved-one to cease
destructive behavior that endangers themselves and others in the family?
Which of us would stand by for sixteen minutes while neighbor kids rode
repeatedly through our freshly landscaped yard on their bikes? Who would
knowingly allow innocents to be violated by lust-driven or rage-filled

perpetrators for even sixteen seconds? Will we, then, with our very, very thin résumé of patience accuse God of lovelessness, and charge Him with being judgmental after 1600 years of forbearance toward our ancestors?

Only in foolishness do we judge God and His judgment.

We have to ask ourselves, why did God eventually bring judgment? Was it simply to register a cosmic point of law? Absolutely not. He was compelled by love. This may be difficult for you to accept initially, but the same relationship-offering love that inspired Creation also triggered judgment. God's longing for fellowship still motivated Him. He never intended to wipe our planet clean—and leave it empty of our race for eternity. He sought to preserve us and our relationship with Him. Consequently, God had only two choices—*replace* humanity with another species, or *restore* us. God chose to redeem humanity, rather than to recreate it.

> **God had only two choices–*replace* humanity with another species, or *restore* us.**

## Judgment with a Promise

Back to history. Through the centuries, a few individuals like Enoch "walked with God,"[18] and were found "blameless."[19] Noah was such a man. He "found favor [grace] in the eyes of the Lord."[20]

Noah was an Old Testament prophet. Perhaps you don't think of him that way because your image of those prophets-of-old is more akin to the picture portrayed by the man outside the church in Athens. But bear with me for a moment. I think it's safe to say that no prophet in the Bible received revelation about more severe judgment than Noah did. His message-from-God was the greatest condemnation and consequence ever to befall our race: the end of the world.

And yet, look at the pattern God established for this judgment-upon-the-world. It contains such an obvious truth—but one that "Holy Hubert" and others like him completely miss: When God declared the end of the world, He simultaneously made a promise for its future. God told Noah about impending judgment, but He also told Noah to build the Ark.

God said, "I'm going to flood the earth; build a boat to survive the flood" (see Genesis 6:14).

When people only read small sections of the Old Testament at a time—and don't grasp the entire story—they miss the simple truth that God's judgments always include promises. Judgments of God invariably contain provisions for deliverance. Condemnation isn't the entire story. God certainly does censure people for their sin, but if you keep reading in your Bible, you will discover that every sentence He declares *against* His people is always accompanied with promises *for* their future. For God, judgment and promise go hand in hand.

Because earthly judgment and a guilty verdict in the courts of man usually end the story, we're often blind to this exciting element in God's form of judgment. When He passes sentence and renders a verdict of guilty, He is *not* finished with us. Much like a physician reaching a conclusive diagnosis about a patient, God specifies our infection/guilt—and begins to treat it. God uses judgment to change people and their destiny.

That process—determining guilt but finding a way to restore the guilty one to innocence—is the essence of redemption. God has been doing that through the ages. Consider, for instance, the years of wandering in the desert that resulted from Israel's presumption and sin. Their wrongdoing lost them an earlier entry into the land He had prepared for them, but He didn't give up on them or stop doing them good! He gave them manna, so they would learn to live on His words—and His end goal was to do them good.[21]

**God's judgment is *not*, primarily, punishment for past behavior, but prelude for future blessing.**

If you view the Old Testament as a process of God redeeming/restoring humanity—instead of just condemning it—you begin to realize that God's judgment has a purpose, a promise. We miss almost everything of

God's intent when we mistakenly view His judgment only as a penalty imposed on His people. God's judgment is not, primarily, punishment for past behavior, but prelude for future blessing.

Does He, at times, correct and punish His kids when they act in a manner that is unworthy of their standing as His children? Yes. But why? God uses conviction and judgment as elements of redemption to restore His people and to change their future for the better.

## Remodeling Process

Let me give you a non-religious example of what I mean. Anyone who has been involved in a remodeling project is well acquainted with the saying, "It always looks worse before it looks better." When my wife and I decided to enlarge our living room (to create more floor space for all our grandkids), it sounded so easy: just move the existing wall on one side of our house five feet over. Very quickly I discovered that (*duh*) all remodeling begins with demolition. You cannot refurbish a bathroom without first removing the old fixtures and tile.

It would have been ridiculous to build a new outer wall without tearing down the old one. But our house looked terrible during the demolition stage. The builders destroyed most of one side of our home, and it was no fun for us. Wouldn't we have sounded silly, though, if we complained about the old wall being removed?

Remodeling begins with removing; old things need to be torn out and torn down before new things get built up. If the contractor did not, also, eventually build a new wall, we could justly accuse him of "wrecking everything." But questioning his integrity during the demolition phase would have been crazy. So it is with people who fail to realize that God is in the process of building a better future for them by removing (dismantling) old attitudes, thoughts, and behaviors. God restores our souls,[22] and a vital aspect of "building us up" is demolishing wrongly constructed strongholds and distortions in our lives.[23] The point of judgment is that it allows God to "restore" and "rebuild" us as we were meant to be.[24]

36

God created a fabulous life for Adam and all his descendants. It was a perfect home. Satan and the *sin-force* destroyed that perfection and ruined what God designed. Unholy powers only know how to tear down. Satan is a thief, a destroyer, a killer;[25] he never rebuilds or restores. Jesus, on the other hand, restores our life and repairs the damage done to us by unrighteousness. He remodels and refurbishes us. He uses His authority and expertise to build us up, not to demolish us.[26]

God is a (re)builder, not a destroyer.

Any conviction that is truly from God is a beginning of something He wants to do for you. God does challenge and correct wrong things in your life. However, when He convicts you of "things that need to go," He isn't giving up on you or writing you off. Quite the contrary, it is because He has a future in mind for you that He marks old walls and fixtures for removal. He is working on you with a set of blueprints that He drafted ages ago.[27] He disciplines, corrects, instructs, and remodels everyone He loves.[28]

What conclusion do you come to as a result of believing those guilty feelings that plague you? Don't they tell you it is too late and that all is lost? Or that God gave you a chance to be different, but you blew the opportunity? The bottom line is that they threaten you with the most horrific and grievous possibility your soul can imagine: *God gives up on you.* Your panic and grief, your worry and anguish about possibly losing your relationship with Jesus is the best proof that you *have not.*

> **Any conviction that is truly from God is a beginning of something He wants to do for you.**

Can someone throw away his or her relationship with God by choosing to no longer have faith? Yes, I believe that is possible. But denying Christ for all eternity is the consequence of unbelief, not misbehavior. We don't lose our salvation because of sins we commit. You and I stand by our faith, and we have been grafted in among God's people because we believe that through Jesus' death on the Cross, Christ atoned for our sins.[29] Our standing is not due to sinlessness, so sinfulness cannot cut salvation out from under us.

However, if former believers consciously elect to not believe, to not accept the offer of forgiveness on the basis of faith in Christ, then I presume they will be "broken off for their unbelief."[30] Let me emphasize—you cannot "lose" your salvation by sinning too badly or too frequently. Salvation is a matter of faith, so unless you consciously choose to renounce your faith in Christ, you are sealed by the Holy Spirit and secure for eternity.[31]

---

1   Romans 1:16; 1 Corinthians 1:18-21
2   Matthew 13:44
3   Ezekiel 44:23
4   2 Corinthians 11:13-15
5   Psalm 68:20
6   Hebrews 2:17-18; 4:15
7   Matthew 8:17
8   John 3:17
9   Ephesians 1:5-8
10  Genesis 1:28, 2:17
11  Genesis 3:7
12  Psalm 101:4
13  Romans 5:12
14  Genesis 4:7
15  Genesis 6:5, 11-12
16  Genesis 6:5
17  Genesis 6:6-7
18  Genesis 5:24
19  Genesis 6:9
20  Genesis 6:8
21  Deuteronomy 8:18ff
22  Psalm 23:3
23  See 2 Corinthians 10:3-8
24  Jeremiah 33:7
25  John 10:10
26  2 Corinthians 10:8
27  Isaiah 25:1
28  Hebrews 12:6
29  Romans 11:17ff
30  Romans 11:20
31  2 Corinthians 1:22; Ephesians 1:13-14; 4:30

# Chapter 4

# Promises and Commands

---

To put in plain words why you and I often feel guilty even after confessing our sins to Jesus, it's necessary to introduce subjects and themes you might have never considered or bothered with before. I realize that you are anxious for answers. My heart's cry is to help free you from condemnation. You plunked down a good chunk of change for this book, and are waiting for me to deliver on what the title and cover promise. My dilemma as a teacher is that I need to talk about some things that won't, at first, seem to answer anything.

We live in a culture that wants "sound bite" answers to huge questions. I'm reminded of a quote widely attributed to Oliver Wendell Holmes: "I would not give a fig for the simplicity this side of complexity, but I would give my life for the simplicity on the other side of complexity." To answer questions, we sometimes have to get to the simplicity on the other side of complexity. Bear with me as I circle back around and come at your question from an entirely different angle.

I'm sure you agree with me that the *whole* story is very important for getting the whole point. Any good story is ruined if the reader stops before finishing it. That is exactly the case with the Old Testament. People end up with wrong conclusions about God—and His doings in the Old Testament—because they pull isolated details of stories from their surroundings, and don't read the stories' conclusions (and beginnings). Many of the episodes in the Old

Testament that seem to reveal a cruel, vengeful, and uncaring God actually demonstrate just the opposite.

Let's start with an often-overlooked truth: the entire nation of Israel was God's witness to the world. They were the collective light to which the nations could come to learn about the Lord.[1] So, it was crucial for them to live according to God's prescribed patterns for life;[2] otherwise, their witness would be distorted by the practices and doctrines of false gods. If they sacrificed their infants to bloodthirsty gods, as the nations around them did, then God would appear no different than those evil-spirited gods.

**Many of the episodes in the Old Testament that seem to reveal a cruel, vengeful, and uncaring God actually demonstrate just the opposite.**

When fundamental wrongness infected the people of God at points in their history, God chose to preserve His witness—and our hope—by eliminating the dangerously infected parts. Much like a surgeon must, at times, cut out a tumor in order to preserve someone's future life, so too did the Lord carefully and completely eliminate cancerous distortions and malignancies from among His people. As a way of preserving the whole nation's future, God removed the influences that would have cut off His people from their future inheritance.

When you read about God's judgment against individuals in Old Testament stories, you may worry that God is going to judge you in the same way. You wonder if you have become so sinful that God will cut you off, too.

It will ease your anxiety if you think of yourself as a nation, populated with thoughts, ideas, feelings, and desires that sometimes lure you away from God's plan for your life. Just as He cut off evil leaders and false prophets from within the whole nation of Israel, so He will do away with hurtful and wicked thoughts that live in your mind and heart. You are not in danger of being completely cut off or condemned in judgment. Instead, God uses His word to "judge the thoughts and intentions of the heart"[3]—applying forgiveness when needed, and exercising spiritual surgery when necessary.

I hope this understanding removes much of your dread about "the God of the Old Testament." He is our Shepherd who leads, feeds, and protects us, and He loves few things more than to bless us in the very presence of our enemies.[4] The evil-spirited and the serpent-of-old want us to believe that God is out to get us—and nail us for our missteps. They paint Him as our adversary, rather than our Advocate, and make Him out as a cruel, easily angered taskmaster.

The truth is that God has set Himself to care for and advantage us, almost in spite of ourselves. Though we make poor followers, like the Children of Israel in the wilderness, He keeps circling back around to pick us up again and get us back on track. That, ultimately, is the purpose for His commands and promises.

## (Very) Few Commands

Let's go back to our history lesson and pick up the timeline where we left off in the last chapter. We learned that the Ark was a promise of *life-after-the-flood*. In the midst of judgment, God promised to preserve Noah, his family, and the animals of the Earth. Noah believed God, and his belief saved our race. So, the pattern we see in God's earliest dealings with our race is that people can be saved from God's judgment by believing a promise He gives to them at the same time He declares judgment upon them. Belief in a promise saves us from judgment.

**Belief in a promise saves us from judgment.**

After the floodwaters subsided, God swore never again to destroy the earth with water, and He marked His covenant with a now-famous rainbow.[5] Despite knowing the evil bent "of man's heart,"[6] God still blessed Noah and his sons, and used them to repopulate "the whole world."[7] He told Noah, "Be fruitful and multiply,"[8]

41

just as He said to Adam 1600 years earlier. Interestingly, however, God did not add many new commandments to spell out "right and wrong." The only commandments He gave Noah were (1) do not eat "flesh with its life, that is, its blood," and (2) do not murder.[9]

During the next four centuries (encapsulated in just two short chapters—Genesis 10-11), Noah's descendants and their extended families became people groups who "separated on the earth."[10] Not once during that era of human expansion did God lay down additional codes of conduct or moral precepts. Think about the time span. Two thousand years since the Garden of Eden, and still God issued almost no commands; He limited His words primarily to blessings and promises.

The *Spirit of the Pharisee* blinds us to this remarkable fact of God's earliest history with humankind. It tries to convince us that God initiated relationship with us using commands and rules for conduct. He did not. As we will see, commandments have never defined God's connection with our race. Our ancestors' future well-being was always the result of God's promises—and their choice to believe in those promises.

> **Commandments have never defined God's connection with our race.**

God told Noah about both the Flood and the Ark. We don't title the episode, "Noah and the Flood" because it isn't ultimately a story about violated commands and judgment; it's an epic message of God's promise and salvation.

## Noah and the Tent

Speaking of stories, I doubt that you ever heard about "Noah and the Tent" in Sunday School. Does it surprise you to learn that shortly after Noah received the rainbow-accented benediction from God, he got drunk?[11] God had issued no commands telling Noah to avoid drunkenness—or warning his youngest son, Ham, away from mocking his father who slept off his drunkenness, sprawled naked in a tent. Noah cursed Ham for his disrespect, but we hear nary a whisper of judgment or consequence from God for Noah's foolishness.

Did Noah feel like he was doing something inappropriate? Possibly. People did have a conscience in those early years of human history, but they had no specific rules to bolster their conscience. They likely felt a convicting uneasiness when they acted in a way that we would call "sinful" today, but no one had a pocket-guide reference-book listing behaviors to avoid. Imagine their disadvantage. Without a moral compass, in the centuries before the Law was given to Moses, each person did whatever they thought was best.[12]

Noah died at the age of 950, remembered by all, not as a drunk, but as the builder of the Ark. I am certain that if the prophet who accosted me in the parking lot in Greece were offered opportunity to travel back in time, he would gladly accept the assignment to declare, "There is sin in this tent." Most of us forget Noah's tent. Instead, we remember his world-preserving belief in God's promise. No amount of after-the-fact drunkenness could jeopardize the salvation Noah had already experienced in the Flood. He believed God. That's what saved him.

> **God's promise to forgive is weightier than our failure to obey.**

## Pointing to the Future

The best way to understand what God ultimately wants to do in your life is to look for His promises. One of the greatest tragedies of people's spiritual walk is that they tend to overlook God's promises—and focus exclusively on His commands. They confuse promises with commands, lumping them together because both are His "word" to us. Unless we grasp how fundamentally dissimilar commands and promises are from one another, we won't understand why God's promise to forgive is weightier than our failure to obey. Commands and promises both point to our future—but in entirely different ways.

## A Future by Commands

Let's first look at how God uses commands to lead us into the best possible future. Think of commands as instructions. If we keep to the instructions for installing new software, for instance, things work; if we fail to follow the outlined steps, the program doesn't run properly. Likewise, if we follow the directions a friend gave us for driving to a party—turning right when told to turn right—we end up at the party. If we miss a turn or intentionally take a wrong turn, the party will go on without us. Commands are God's way of guiding us every day so that we arrive at His good intent for our tomorrow.

Planet earth was broken by the *sin-force*, as though torn up by a massive earthquake.[13] The world no longer works the way God designed it. Everything about life has been moved off-center. Without directions it's now easy to lose our way, so God provides commands, like signposts, to warn us away from treacherous passages, dead-ends, and impassable road-ways. His commands get us around and through life's psycho-spiritual obstacles and danger-places. Commands lead us in "the path of life," and when we follow that trail, we end up living in "pleasant places," suited for and satisfied with our "heritage."[14]

The point of commands is guidance, not judgment. Walking by His statutes ensures life in the midst of a spiritually dead and dying world.[15]

Satan has been a liar from the beginning. In the Garden of Eden, he challenged God's words and sought to convince our ancestors that God's motive for commanding Adam and Eve not to eat the fruit was to withhold good—not to give it. The serpent claimed God was limiting their enjoyment and fulfillment. No wonder, then, that the "*Spirit of the Pharisee*" tries to do the same. That lying god adds a false flavor to God's commands, causing them to feel restrictive, compulsory, rigid, and unsympathetic.

But if God's commands are a set of directions to get from where we are to a fabulous destination, don't we want them to be clear? What good is a set of directions that don't give direction? Strangers driving through an unfamiliar city want someone to tell them precisely how to get to their destination. *Go three blocks and make a sharp right turn just after the light (not onto the street with the light)*, doesn't offend them; it enables them to get where they want to go.

Too many of us view God's commands as traffic barriers that force us to detour. Actually, they are like a GPS navigation system in our car telling us when and where to turn. God's instructions are designed to help, not threaten us. Is there a consequence for disregarding His instructions for life? Yes. All sin leads to some form of death; which is to say, sin cuts us off from a future that otherwise would have been ours, and it severs us to some degree from right connections with others.

One thing that is true of us all is that we often imagine we know a better destination—one that will satisfy us more than the place God is leading us to—or, that we know a "shortcut" that isn't in His directions. Destinations and directions that aren't in God's plan may seem right and good to us, but they are not. They are deadly to us in one way or another.[16] They always diminish our person and/or our spiritual inheritance on earth.

Some commands spell out specific consequences-for-good that will be our portion if we obey. For instance, God urges us to "honor" father and mother because doing so will "prolong" our days "in the land which the Lord [our] God gives [us]."[17] These commands are like equations: "If you do X, the result will be Y." Based on our response to His commands, we experience either advantage or loss. If we pay attention to the commands—and do them—our well-being will continue "like a river," and blessing will wash against us again and again like ocean waves.[18]

**Commands are meant to reduce the amount of loss we suffer and incease the degree of delight we enjoy in life.**

45

Commands are meant to reduce the amount of loss we suffer and increase the degree of delight we enjoy in life. Obedience and disobedience radically affect our future. Obedience always leads to a better future than disobedience. Everyone who keeps God's ways—the instructions He lays out—will "be blessed,"[19] well-guided, and prosperous of soul.[20]

## A Future by Promises

Like God's commands, His promises connect us with future blessing, but in an entirely different manner. His commands and blessings don't conflict with one another; but they are two distinct avenues through which He does our race good.

Because I was in Athens, I used an analogy my audience could relate to. I said, "I love all the activity of your city. Walking to and from my apartment to the church is an adventure. The food is fabulous. The people are friendly. The blend of ancient and modern architecture is unlike anywhere I have visited before." I paused for a moment then continued more slowly, "Athens traffic, however, is *interesting . . .*"

They nodded enthusiastically and grinned as though I had discovered their secret. I then inquired off-handedly, "Could you give me directions for how to drive to the Acropolis from here?"

Everyone just stared at me. I interpreted their silence as a *Yes*.

"What would you estimate my chances are to successfully drive myself to the Acropolis, using your directions?"

Polite silence.

"You think I'd get lost, don't you—even with your directions? And let me guess, you don't think your directions are the problem?"

A loud silence.

"Would you recommend a taxi, instead?"

They smiled and nodded like parents watching a child's first faltering steps.

A promise from God is like a taxi in Athens. Regardless of my personal ability to navigate the drive to the Acropolis in a car of my own, the taxi will get me there. My driving skills and familiarity with road signs in Athens are completely beside the point. A taxi is a great equalizer because no taxi passenger's skill and experience in driving distinguishes him or her from the rest of us. Calling someone a good or bad driver when they aren't driving is meaningless. Likewise, referring to people as good or bad—when they are relying on the promise of God—is moot.

God wants to ensure His people come into their inheritance, and He doesn't want to depend on our limited abilities to get us there. Our strength-of-will to follow His commands is too unreliable. We readily cave in to temptation. We give in to distracting impulses. Like the people of Israel on the way to the Promised Land centuries ago, we perpetually misinterpret God's arrangements, and grumble against His instructions.[21]

As if those vulnerabilities are not problem enough, think of how utterly foreign the spiritual world is from the natural world. Like Athens is to a California boy, the hazards and happenings of the spiritual realm are incomprehensible to our natural perception—and we don't know the meaning of any of the road signs.[22] The chances for a natural person to arrive at a spiritual destination are slim, indeed. Having a taxi driver with lots of local knowledge is far, far better than having a set of directions to follow.

So, in addition to commands—in fact long before He instituted the Law—God provided fail-safe promises for our ultimate future. Promises have always been the first and best means for transporting us to God's planned destination. God knows we believe better than we behave. Whose behavior has been the most consistent in your life—yours or God's? If you had to rely on one or the other, whose capability to keep God's words would you choose? With your eternal destiny on the line, upon whose performance would you stake everything? I bet on His promises and His promise to keep to His own words.

**Promises have always been the first and best means for transporting us to God's planned destination.**

## Responding to Commands and Promises

Let me emphasize again that God intends blessing for us. He is our Shepherd, and He pursues us with "goodness and loving-kindness" all the days of our lives—both through commands and promises.[23]

Intuitively, we respond differently to commands than to promises: we *obey* commands, but we *believe* promises. Obeying and believing are closely related. *Having faith* and *being obedient* often go hand-in-hand, so it is understandable that we mix them up sometimes. But it is nonsensical to obey a promise—to try fulfilling it on our own. Obeying a promise is a contradiction in terms. When God promises, only He can execute it. Promises rely on God's behavior, not ours. The Promise-Maker is the Promise-Keeper.

> **We (usually) keep His commands; God (always) keeps His promises.**

We (usually) keep His commands; God (always) keeps His promises.

Knowing we will be frustrated by our fleshy attempts, the *Spirit of the Pharisee* urges us to do what Abraham and Sarah tried to do while waiting for God to keep His promise. When the promised child didn't come as quickly as they thought it should, Abraham and Sarah tried to do God's work for Him by joining Abraham to Hagar. Their own-flesh efforts produced a child-of-the-flesh. That is all any attempt to obey a promise can bring into being. Their surrogate actions could never fulfill God's promise. Ishmael could never be Isaac: one was born "according to the flesh," while the other was born "through the promise."[24]

## Love and Obedience

As I said earlier, faith in God's promises is often closely linked with obedience to His commands, but when we try to obey a promise, we are ultimately functioning in our flesh. Trying to obey a promise will only produce an

Ishmael, a child-of-the-flesh. So, if our salvation is a promise to believe—and not a command to obey—where does obedience fit in God's plan for our life?

I will be saying many things about obedience as the book progresses, and I'm purposefully not giving you a short, simple answer because I need to unpack all the baggage and misunderstanding that people have about obedience before I explain its purpose. For now, let me talk about a verse that is often quoted as a proof-text by those who insist that what Jesus wants most from you is obedience: "If you love Me, you will keep my commandments."[25] The *Spirit of the Pharisee* misuses this verse and turns it into a backwards equation: "If you don't keep my commandments, it proves that you don't love me."

Jesus was assuring His friends that love leads to obedience. God's love inspires His promises; His promises inspire our love and faith, which in turn inspire our obedience to His commands. But that Kingdom dynamic does not necessarily work in reverse. Increasing the level of morality in someone's life will not necessarily increase his or her love for Jesus. More love for God inspires more obedience to Him, but greater obedience does not necessarily lead to greater love.

> **More love for God inspires more obedience to Him, but greater obedience does not necessarily lead to greater love.**

This is one reason why some people—especially those who feel like they "have done everything right" in their relationship with God—do not necessarily feel intimacy with Him. The *Spirit of the Pharisee* takes advantage of their sincere, but misguided, efforts. It tells them that the reason they do not feel close to God, and do not feel His love for them, is because they are unworthy and disobedient. If they simply "worked harder" at being obedient, they would feel more love.

Not true. Keeping God's commands will not motivate us to love Him more.

As I taught that night in Athens, I flashed back to several particular people I have known through the years whose spiritual life emitted an air of frustration and rigidity. They felt defrauded and cheated when they

49

"lived right," but didn't necessarily feel greater intimacy with God. Their heightened, almost frantic need to be/do right (in order to gain favor and intimacy with God), made them critical of themselves—and others. Deep down, they were angry. They judged God as unfair because they held to their end of the deal but He didn't. They obeyed Him, so why didn't they enjoy a more intimate and personable relationship with Him?

We cannot earn God's love.

He is not our taskmaster;[26] He is our Father.[27] God promises a love-relationship with us. When we confuse roles—and try to maintain intimate connection with Him by "keeping" His commands—we alter the basis of the relationship. Instead of relying on and resting in His promise to be our God, we take upon ourselves the obligation to "live up to" (i.e. be good enough for) a relationship with Him. That is completely backward. First, our hearts learn to call God *Abba*,[28] and then as a consequence of that established intimacy, we yearn to do the things that please Him.

> **Moral codes are not letters of affection. Neither are they adoption papers.**

Trying to please Him before we know we are adopted into a child-Father relationship almost never leads to a settled sense of love between us. We try to make ourselves (more) deserving of His favor. And fail. Guides for thought and conduct are important, but they are not the basis for our relationship with God. Moral codes are not letters of affection. Neither are they adoption papers. Even perfect obedience will not sustain the love-relationship founded on His promises.

Isn't much of the guiltiness you feel mostly about your failure to live up to a standard of obedience? You have come up short. It seems so right, doesn't it, to presume that you have lost connection with God because separation from God is the just desserts for "bad" Christians? But those feelings are based on a terrible and unscriptural notion: "If I am a good person, God will love me more; if I am bad, He will love me less."

Such conditional love may have been your experience in life—among family or friends—but God loves us unconditionally. He doesn't evaluate our goodness and love us corresponding to how well we behave. Trying to generate love through obedience is a dead-end road. Those who attempt to maintain intimate connection to God exclusively by keeping His commands will be sorely disappointed. They're going about it all wrong.

God wants our love first, knowing our obedience will follow after.

---

1. Isaiah 60:3ff
2. See Deuteronomy 4:1-8
3. Hebrews 4:12
4. See Psalm 23
5. Genesis 9:13
6. Genesis 8:21
7. Genesis 9:17-22
8. Genesis 9:1
9. Genesis 9:4, 6
10. Genesis 10:32
11. Genesis 9:20ff
12. Deuteronomy 12:8
13. Isaiah 24:5-6, 19-20
14. Psalm 16:6, 11
15. Ezekiel 33:11ff
16. Proverbs 14:12
17. Exodus 20:12; see also Ephesians 6:2
18. Isaiah 48:17-18
19. Psalm 128:1; Proverbs 8:32
20. Deuteronomy 29:9
21. Numbers 14:2
22. 1 Corinthians 2:14; see also 13:12
23. Psalm 23:6
24. Galatians 4:23
25. John 14:15
26. Hosea 2:16
27. Romans 8:15
28. Galatians 4:6

# Chapter 5

# A Remnant and a Reckoning

I first heard the expression, "All that glitters is not gold," as a young boy growing up near Placerita Canyon about thirty miles north of Los Angeles. Gold was discovered in Placerita Canyon in 1842—nearly six years before the more-famous discovery at Sutter's Mill further north in California. As the story goes, a man named Francisco Lopez dug up some wild onions with his knife and found gold nuggets entangled in their roots. Consequently, all us locals took great pride in the historic and geologic significance of our area. As kids we went on school field trips to "pan for gold," and we learned about the features of terrain early prospectors sought out in their quest for the best place to "sink a mine."

Naturally, youngsters in our community hoped to find gold as we trekked through the countryside. My friends and I were disappointed more than once. After lugging sparkling rocks home in our pockets, sure of our wealth and good fortune, we discovered that we had discovered nothing of value. Our big "finds" were iron or copper pyrite, otherwise known as "fool's gold." The lesson stuck with me: not all rocks are created equal.

I offer that object lesson in the hope that you will realize much of the condemnation and fear you lug around in your heart might look like God's judgment against you and your sin, but it isn't true judgment—at least, not judgment from the true God who loves you.

The elements composing God's judgment are as different from those in our natural concept of judgment as gold is from pyrite. Unfortunately, our lack of understanding about true, spiritual judgment leaves us more vulnerable than we need to be to those guilty feelings that sometimes hang around after we confess and repent of our behavior. If you want to unload the false stones that weigh you down, if you would like to rid yourself of "Fool's Judgment," there are several unusual aspects of God's judgment you should know.

> **Our lack of understanding about true, spiritual judgment leaves us more vulnerable than we need to be.**

## Judgment and Deliverance

As I have hinted all along, God's judgment inherently provides a means of deliverance for His people—the ones under judgment. Like a warning trumpet blown by a watchman to alert people that a destroying force is coming against them, God's judgment comes in two parts.[1] Israel's perpetual sin and apostasy did lead, in many instances, to punishing judgments from God—when He scattered them away from their spiritual inheritance and allowed them to live under the dominion of cruel taskmasters. They sometimes learned their lessons the hard way. But before the "avenging sword" arrived, God announced its arrival. His judgment is like lightning and thunder: first comes the warning, followed by an interval of time before the thunder. God's judgment first presents us with an opportunity to escape; we don't hear thunder without lightning.

Except in the case of what we call the "Final Judgment," God's judgment makes a gracious way of salvation available for His children to be brought back and restored from the consequences of their sin.[2] God did judge His people for their sins, but because they were His people, "He became their Savior."[3] He redeems "with an outstretched arm and with great judgments."[4] His arm brings both judgment and salvation.[5] That's why He was "astonished" when no one could be found to "help" or "uphold" those under judgment.[6]

God, who judges righteously, is also "mighty to save."[7] Read your Bible carefully, and you will see this pattern again and again: Judgment and deliverance are companions, not disconnected activities.[8] Consequently, if the condemnation and disqualification you feel as a result of your sin does not point you toward a clear opportunity for redemption and rescue, you can be sure that the Author of your salvation is not the author of those horrid, death-dealing feelings![9]

> **Judgment and deliverance are companions, not disconnected activities.**

By the way, a curious detail about all the deliverers God raised up through the ages is that they always came from among the very people He judged. That is why Jesus had to become flesh—and dwell among us.[10] Jesus is the Anointed One, sent by God to "proclaim release to the captives."[11] But to be our Deliverer, Jesus needed to be part of our race. "He had to be made like His brethren in all things;"[12] otherwise, He wouldn't qualify as a Deliverer to atone for the sins of humanity.

## Judgment and Mercy

Mercy is imbedded in God's judgment. That is another telltale feature of true judgment. God is merciful,[13] and His mercy is over all His works—even His judgment.[14] Everyone instinctively longs for a merciful God. It's why some of your unbelieving friends have probably asked you, "If God is so loving and merciful, how could He send people to hell for their sins?" Unfortunately, the question presumes that mercy and judgment are mutually exclusive, unconnected actions. Such an either/or perspective supposes that a God who is merciful cannot judge. By their definition, therefore, a blanket pardon must be expected from a merciful God.

Even well-intentioned church leaders get tripped up by this either/or mentality, and have a hard time reconciling the God who loves with the God who judges. Some teachers try to resolve their conflicted ideas by theorizing that love/mercy will move God to suspend all judgment. They suggest that though God has laid down rules of conduct, in the end His love will force Him to relent—and accept everyone into eternity, regardless of what they've done. Frankly, that is heresy, and it renders Christ's death on the Cross an unnecessary and arbitrary gesture by a God who knows the future well enough to know if He is going to issue a blanket pardon at the end of time.

**Neither mercy-without-judgment nor judgment-without-mercy are God's plan.**

The reason that universal salvation—and by that, I refer to the teaching that everyone will go to heaven—gains a hearing even in the Church is because we know God's love personally, and we know how much He has forgiven us. Why would God not do the same for others (i.e. everyone) if He has shown such loving mercy to us?

Neither mercy-without-judgment nor judgment-without-mercy are God's plan. We judge God's judgment unfairly when we strip it of mercy, and we likewise misinterpret His mercy if we remove it from judgment. Mercy and judgment are inseparable companions in the Kingdom of God, under its rule and government. With a natural concept of judgment, that seems almost nonsensical. Mercy and judgment at the same time? Aren't those mutually exclusive and opposite concepts? How can that be?

**A Remnant**

The key to this difficult-to-grasp aspect of God's judgment is the basis upon which He extends mercy. This is the point over which many people stumble, but it is a perfect picture of how the Law and Grace work together, and it explains some of why you and I struggle with lingering regret and shame. What is the mechanism for mercy-in-judgment? What is everyone's hope for escape from final judgment?

Those questions lead us to another fascinating and encouraging aspect of God's judgment. Reading through the Old Testament we discover that God never judges an entire group without delivering some of the group. His judgments are not wholesale, indiscriminate, or all-inclusive. There are always some who escape judgment, and the escaping group is known as the "remnant."[15]

The entire nation of Israel was judged many times for their sin-acts, and God scattered His people throughout the nations. In each instance, however, He promised to "leave a remnant."[16] The remnant always survived exile and "captivity,"[17] and God kept them "alive by a great deliverance."[18] The remnant consistently received "less than [their] iniquities deserve."[19] Due to God's "unchanging love," He passed over "the rebellious act of the remnant,"[20] much like the Angel of Death passed over the homes marked by the blood of the Passover lamb. Though He condemned the sins of the nation, He cast the sins of the remnant into "the depths of the sea."[21]

**It wasn't our goodness, but God's graciousness that set us free from the judgement.**

How is the remnant chosen? Curiously, God does not select members of the remnant based on their works or behavior; rather, they are picked simply by God's "gracious choice."[22] The remnant is "saved,"[23] as an expression of "grace."[24] In the midst of judgment—grace. A remnant saved, delivered, preserved. That is the pattern God arranged for judgment from the very beginning.

As a follower of Christ, you are one of the remnant. The apostle Paul calls you and me "vessels of mercy," a "remnant" to whom God made "known the riches of His glory."[25] His gracious choice makes believers-in-Christ a remnant.[26] It wasn't our goodness, but God's graciousness that set us free from the judgment we deserve. You might say, God makes a new people in the midst of all the people of the earth. All of us who choose to trust in Jesus' sacrifice become part of that new people group—a remnant unto God. We become the "people of God," a distinct and unusual "race" differentiated from all others by the fact that we "received mercy"![27]

Do you realize what that means—and what freedom it offers? Since you were not included in the remnant on the basis of your good behavior, neither will you be excluded from the remnant on the basis of your bad behavior. That's what Paul means when he says God chose each of us: "by grace . . . [not] on the basis of works, otherwise grace is no longer grace."[28]

## Promise of Mercy

As I pointed out before, everyone intuitively longs for a merciful God. That's because He intentionally fashioned people to look for mercy and cry out for rescue when doom or disaster approach. Subconsciously, every person hopes to escape punishment, to be part of the remnant that receives mercy. The *Spirit of the Pharisee* lies and tells us that the way to become part of the remnant is to work harder at being more obedient to the Law. We promise God we "will never do those things again," because we mistakenly believe that our hope for mercy is tied to our obedience.

It isn't.

Mercy is tied to promises—and faith. The Law "is not of faith,"[29] so it is foolish to trust in obedience to the Law to gain access into the remnant. If obedience to the Law could gain us access to the remnant, then disobedience would force us out.

Pause for a moment to think back on your attempts to appease God after you were deeply convicted about sin. Somewhere in the midst of your regret and remorse, didn't you promise Him you wouldn't commit that sin again? Did you tell Him you had learned your lesson and wouldn't be so foolish in the future?

Leaving aside the question of whether or not you kept that promise, I doubt that even in your most sincere and earnest moments of repentance you told God you would never commit *any* sin ever again. That would be too much to promise—too much for even you to believe about yourself. A sinless life? Preposterous for any of us to propose.

Unfortunately, that places us right back in a guilty position because even though we might manage to straighten up our lives in a few particulars, we still mess up in others. If we are or will be guilty of even one infraction, we are law-breakers and guilty as before.[30] That is why the way of escape, the pathway of redemption provided by God is not through the Law. God doesn't show us mercy in the midst of judgment because we promise to do a better job of obeying, but because, like Abraham, we keep believing in God's promise. The mechanism for mercy is God's gracious choice to save those who call on His name.[31]

> **The mechanism for mercy is God's gracious choice to save those who call on His name.**

God says of the remnant, "Just as you were a curse among the nations . . . I will save you that you may become a blessing."[32] Those under a curse saved to become a blessing. Sound familiar?

Infected by the *sin-force*, you and I were under the curse of "original sin," as well as under the curse of laws we violated.[33] In what way could such sinful, cursed people be a blessing to others? We are prophetic messengers to the world because we are justified by faith and not by a perfect record of obedience. From the onset of human history, God planned to "justify the Gentiles by faith," so He introduced "the gospel beforehand to Abraham, saying, 'All the nations will be blessed through you.' "[34]

That is what God is like: He grants mercy in Jesus' name to terrible sinners who, by all rights under the Law, deserve judgment and punishment. Then He uses those forgiven and pardoned sinners to "proclaim the excellencies of Him who called [them] out of darkness into His marvelous light."[35] We spread the good news of His mercy-in-judgment.

## A Reckoning

In the previous chapter, we learned about God's promises—and how His promises hold the key to everything He does for us. It's time to begin connecting some of the dots in our discussion to see why those feelings of banishing shame and hopeless reproach are not God's word to you. Promises are like taxis in Athens—remember? You and I are more guaranteed to arrive at God's intentions for us if we rely on the taxi driver and not in our own ability to navigate the signs and streets in a foreign city.

**Abraham's story recalibrated the entire world because it marked the earliest appearance of an antidote to the *sin-force*.**

The pivotal promise in the Old Testament, and the one that figures most prominently in our discussion about the Law and Grace, was given to Abram more than 400 years after Noah built the Ark. Even though it gets ahead of the story, I'll call him Abraham—the name by which we know him today.[36] Abraham's story recalibrated the entire world because it marked the earliest appearance of an antidote to the *sin-force*.

Abraham was the eldest son of Terah, and he lived with his wife, Sarah (Sarai) in modern-day Iraq. He moved with his father and barren wife to Haran along the trade route from Nineveh (remember Jonah?) to Ebla, Damascus, and Canaan. Later, God called Abraham to leave his father's house in Haran, and vowed that He would make Abraham a blessing to "all the families of the earth."[37] His descendants would outnumber the stars visible in the sky.[38]

Quite an astounding promise. Strikingly, God attached no moral or religious conditions to the promise. He gave no law, no commands for Abraham to follow. God didn't proclaim, "If you are good, I will bless you." That lack of behavioral conditions is especially noteworthy because Abraham's moral track record was spotty—at best. Before receiving the world-changing promise, He lied (easily and repeatedly) to protect himself and his interests,[39] and he exploited his wife's physical attractiveness to gain favor with important people.

No one would call Abraham an exceptionally good man. Nevertheless, God chose him to bless the world—without giving him lots of instruction for reforming his behavior.

Almost 25 years would elapse before the promise from God materialized in the birth of Isaac, and during that stretch of time, Abraham and Sarah's patience grew thin. The long delay may be why, more than once, God needed to reinforce His promise. Finally, when Abraham was 99 years old, God told him to change his wife's name to "Princess" because the time had arrived for her to become a "mother of nations."[40]

> **No one would call Abraham an exceptionally good man. Nevertheless, God chose him to bless the world.**

After so many years—too many for his body—Abraham "fell on his face and laughed."[41] *Our bodies are a bit too old for that,* he thought to himself. When he finally recovered from the ridiculousness of God's statement, Abraham responded, "You must mean to bless us through Ishmael."

"No," God corrected him emphatically, "Sarah your wife will bear you a son . . . and I will establish My covenant with him for an everlasting covenant for his descendants after him."[42] God visited Abraham some weeks later to finalize the promise. He declared that within one year, Sarah would give birth to a boy. Sarah, who was listening through the tent-flap, had her own doubts. Like her husband, she "laughed to herself, saying, *Shall I indeed bear a child, when I am so old?*"[43] She, too, struggled with the impossible-sounding promise.

By the grace of God, Abraham finally settled the question that lies at the heart of our spiritual life, and at the root of the doubts and fears that plague us: Can the Promise-Maker keep His word even when I cannot? "With respect to the promise of God, he did not waver in unbelief but grew strong in faith."[44] Abraham's belief—his choice to trust God's faithfulness more than nature's evidence—was "reckoned to him as righteousness."[45]

**Spiritual Etymology**

I know history is challenging enough. As soon as I start in on things like etymology and definitions, I risk losing your attention completely. But

I'm not kidding when I tell you that this is the key to everything related to Grace and the Law. Etymology is the study of the origins of words; it's like history for words—especially focused on how words have arrived at their current meaning, and what words have historical connection with one another in different languages. Sounds boring, huh?

My interest (and soon yours) is in spiritual etymology because God connects words in His vocabulary that we don't think to put together in ours. God "reckons" things differently than humans do, and that difference keeps tripping us up. To show you what I mean, let me ask you a question—it's not a trick question. Don't think about your answer, just give your first/natural response: "Do you call Person X righteous because that person *behaves* or *believes* correctly?"

> **In God's mind, righteousness is determined by what we believe, not how we behave.**

Most of us—especially those of us who sincerely want to be "more" righteous— assume that righteousness is determined by behavior: the more that we act correctly and avoid doing anything wrong, the more righteous we presume we are. But in God's mind, righteousness is determined by what we *believe*, not how we *behave*.

This is a game-changer.

Frankly, our behavior—even our good behavior—has never been very impressive to God. Because of the way our culture speaks about "being good" and "being righteous," it is difficult for us to accept the baseline judgments in the Bible. But God's word tells us "there is none righteous, not even one"; "there is none who does good, there is not even one."[46] From His vantage point, "all of us have become like one who is unclean, and all our righteous deeds are like a filthy garment."[47]

There are no "good people." That is the baseline of morality in God's perspective. Though we like to imagine that we still have opportunity to prove we're good, righteous people, God tells us it's too late to change the verdict on our lives. *Sin-force* symptoms have sapped us dry. Each of us has withered "like a leaf, and our iniquities, like the wind, take us away." A leaf blown from a branch has lost its hope of life.

That is what most readers miss, and it's why we misunderstand so much about our standing before God. Our entire mindset is built around the notion that what we do or don't do determines how righteous we are. God knew that evaluating our track record would leave us without hope. Consequently, He made an entirely different arrangement, a pathway to righteousness for people with an already-established track record of disobedience. God made a new way to righteousness through faith.

The great lesson from early Bible history is not found in humankind's behavior, but in God's.

## A New Reckoning

In Hebrew, to *reckon* (*châshab*) means to *value one item as another, to equate two objects*. Picture two strands of fiber interwoven so completely they become *one-and-the-same*. The two are as one. In God's eyes, faith and righteousness are virtually indistinguishable from one another. Spiritually speaking, they're made of the same stuff.

In New Testament Greek, *to reckon* is translated *logizomai*, to "*take an inventory* and *make an estimate*." This is closer to our English concept of *reckon*, which is to *compute or count up—especially in a final tally*. Someone counts and *translates* one thing into something else, usually its value. For instance, a real estate appraiser *reckons* or *estimates* the value of a piece of property, converting dirt into dollars. The piece of property is worth say $50,000, but you could dig everywhere on the property without finding an actual roll of dollars in the sum of $50,000.

Essentially, that's what God did. He evaluated the (spiritual) significance of Abraham's belief, and *credited* righteousness to his account. God translated faith into righteousness. A plot of dirt and a wad of dollar bills aren't composed of identical molecular structures, yet they are identical in the financial world. In exactly the same way, righteousness and faith may not look alike, but they are identical in the spiritual world.

God reckons faith—belief in a promise—equal (in value) to righteousness.

There wasn't a trace of behavioral righteousness in Abraham's belief. I do not mean his belief was immoral, but Abraham wasn't resisting temptation. His belief had nothing to do with obeying a commandment because the Ten Commandments and the Law didn't even exist at that time. Nevertheless, God computed/equated/translated Abraham's belief as righteousness. That spiritual accounting procedure changed the world.

> **God reckons faith-belief in a promise-equal (in value) to righteousness.**

If Abraham had done something to justify himself—some feat of goodness or a great moral accomplishment—it would make sense for God to pay him a wage of righteousness. But that would have set up an impossible pay scale for humanity. God did not tally up what was due to Abraham for long hours of obedient behavior. Instead, God reckoned Abraham's belief as righteousness, and made salvation a free gift.[48]

Forever onward, *believing*, not *behaving*, was the one and only possible pathway to righteousness.

## Wages or Gift?

*What?*, I guessed my Greek audience was thinking that night in Athens. It's the same reaction we all have to such a notion. When I teach on these concepts, I must find ways to practically explain just how counter-intuitive God's equation for righteousness is to our way of thinking.

*Money*, I thought suddenly, as I stood staring at my translator who was waiting for me to speak. *Everybody understands money. I'll try a money analogy to better explain the most important spiritual equation in the Old Testament.* When I finally broke the uncomfortable silence by saying, "Think of 'righteousness' as a large sum of money equal to a lifetime's wages," everyone, including Angela, refocused their attention.

Workers earn a salary. The money someone gets after working a job is not "credited as a favor, but as what is due."[49] On the other hand, if someone receives money,[50] it can't really be called an (earned) salary; it's a "(free) gift."[51] Spiritually speaking, our salvation is a gift, not a salary. We did not and cannot earn it by working hard. Our labors of obedience never add up to an adequate wage of perfection; and yet, God grants us full forgiveness (translate that: perfection) through Jesus' work on our behalf.

> **Spiritually speaking, our salvation is a gift, not a salary. We did not and cannot earn it by working hard.**

Righteousness is only possible as a free gift from God. Commands have no real power to make anyone righteous because even if we obey them perfectly, no amount of obedience-after-the-fact has the spiritual power to erase our past disobedience—or original sin. Abraham didn't earn his righteousness by doing good works and being obedient to (some) commands (while being disobedient to others). Neither do we.

Our natural inclination is to "make up" for things we have done wrong. We try to compensate for past mistakes by being "extra good from now on." If we feel bad about offending someone with an unkind remark, we intentionally go out of our way to be nice to them over the next few days. We fix things between others and ourselves by correcting our behavior and being extra careful to treat them opposite from how we did before.

Not surprisingly, we try the same approach with God. We promise to be more obedient in the future, and hope He won't judge us for what we have done in the past. We miss the point that our righteousness is a gift, not a paycheck. We do not gain/lose our righteousness by succeeding/failing as obedient workers.

God's earliest dealings with His people were exclusively grounded in covenant promises, not commandments. By His Creator-right and power, God decreed that righteousness comes "on the basis of faith" in His promises.[52] God justifies people not by their obedience to a set of commands, but "by faith."[53] We are a remnant through *believing*—not *obeying*. Our access to God and passing forever out of judgment is through promises—not commands.

The *Spirit of the Pharisee* is a liar because it insists that the only sure way into God's favor is by better behavior and a more spotless track record. Legalism threatens you by saying that because of your sin, there is little hope for God's forgiveness. It instructs you to hang your head and mumble, "I'll try harder."

> **God's earlist dealings with His people were exclusively grounded in covenant promises, not commandments.**

God, on the other hand, is your "glory, and the One who lifts [your] head."[54] Cry to Him and He will answer for "salvation belongs to the Lord," and His blessing is upon His people.[55]

---

1. Ezekiel 33:1ff
2. Deuteronomy 30:4; Jeremiah 29:10-14, 33:25-26
3. Isaiah 63:8
4. Exodus 6:6
5. Isaiah 33:22
6. Isaiah 59:16; 63:5
7. Isaiah 63:1b
8. Isaiah 51:5; 52:10
9. Hebrews 2:10; 12:2
10. John 1:14 (See also Deuteronomy 18:15, 18; Acts 3:22; 7:37)
11. Luke 4:18
12. Hebrews 2:17
13. Psalm 86:15; Luke 6:36
14. Psalm 145:9; James 2:13
15. Ezra 9:13
16. Ezekiel 6:8
17. Nehemiah 1:3
18. Genesis 45:7
19. Ezra 9:13
20. Micah 7:18
21. Micah 7:19
22. Romans 11:5
23. Romans 9:27

24  Ezra 9:8
25  Romans 9:23-29
26  Romans 11:5
27  1 Peter 2:9-10
28  Romans 11:6
29  Galatians 3:12
30  James 2:10-11
31  Joel 2:32
32  Zechariah 8:13
33  Galatians 3:10, 13
34  Galatians 3:8
35  1 Peter 2:9
36  Genesis 17:5
37  Genesis 12:1-4
38  Genesis 15:5
39  See Genesis 12:10ff; Genesis 20:1-7
40  Genesis 17:15-16
41  Genesis 17:17
42  Genesis 17:19
43  Genesis 18:10-13
44  Romans 4:20
45  Romans 4:3; James 2:23
46  Romans 3:10, 12
47  Isaiah 64:6
48  Ephesians 2:8
49  Romans 4:4
50  Romans 4:5
51  Romans 6:23
52  Philippians 3:9
53  Romans 3:28
54  Psalm 3:3
55  Psalm 3:8ff

# Chapter 6

# Cutting Away and Falling Away

---

The stories and conversations in the Old Testament are intentionally "written for our instruction,"[1] so God invites us to read the episodes not merely for an accurate glimpse of history, but also to extract principles and understandings about the invisible realm. For example, God delivered His people from Egypt by the hand of Moses; that is history. But Moses made choices that enabled him to become a deliverer, and he learned lessons along the way. Moses' experiences serve as excellent training for our own journey and ministry. God's long-ago work in and through a man provides us with foundational understanding in the Kingdom.

Likely, you have seen a good mystery movie, and the first time you watched, you didn't notice all the hints that pointed to the eventual outcome. When you watched it a second or third time, the clues were obvious and you wonder how you missed them. That is essentially what New Testament writers say about the Old Testament.[2]

Once you know what to look for, you can spot the Gospel throughout the Old Testament. Salvation and reconciliation with God through faith was "promised long years ago."[3] Though the "mystery" was "hidden" until the full revelation of Christ, the pathway to salvation has been foreshadowed and prophesied "from of old."[4] But the Old Testament record does not necessarily explain everything.

For instance, it doesn't tell us how men like Enoch or Noah pleased God. Because of this, many of us have the misconception that the early heroes of the Bible managed to live perfect, sinless lives. It isn't until we read the New Testament that we discover neither Adam nor his descendants found favor with God on the basis of their sinlessness. The men-of-old were NOT good enough (morally speaking) to be welcomed by God. Rather, they attained righteousness by believing God.

> **It was then–and is now–simply impossible to please God without faith.**

It was then—and is now—simply impossible to please God without faith.[5] Our spiritual heroes and ancestors "gained [God's] approval" by faith:[6] "By faith Abel offered to God a better sacrifice than Cain";[7] Enoch was "taken up" because his faith was "pleasing to God";[8] and, Noah "became an heir of the righteousness which is according to faith."[9] He was judged righteous because he chose to believe (not behave).[10]

## Circumcision

Reading the whole of the Bible, not just isolated parts, enables us to see the consistency of God's dealings with His people over the entire stretch of time. In fact, even elements that don't seem to correlate with one another on first reading, actually do when you set them side by side with the historical record. One such example is circumcision—the unusual mark that many believers associate almost exclusively with Moses and the Law. But it is more about righteousness through promise than by command.

Circumcision seems like a curious way to mark the faith covenant between God and Abraham, but it makes perfect sense if we remember the difference between faith and obedience, between promises and commands. To explain what I mean, let's return to the story of Abraham and Sarah.

As I explained earlier, they confused a promise with a command, and instead of letting God fulfill His promise, they tried to fulfill it themselves. They believed God, but eventually felt that they needed to help Him with the promise. Sound familiar? Believers like you and me have been making that mistake for centuries. Abraham and Sarah came up with an alternate plan for Abraham to father a son through Sarah's maidservant. That was not God's plan. Their plan entailed no faith, just flesh; no belief, just biology.

**Their plan entailed no faith, just flesh; no belief, just biology.**

God didn't need (or want) Abraham's flesh to achieve His purpose.

The 25 years between the promise and its fulfillment eliminated even the remotest possibility that Abraham and Sarah could have a child on their own. When Abraham fathered Isaac, he became the "heir of the world" not "through the Law, but through the righteousness of faith" in God's word.[11] God also gave the "Father of faith" a sign of the covenant-pledge, an indication like the rainbow that pointed to God's promise, not people's performance. Abraham and his offspring were to be circumcised.[12]

The removal of that fleshy fold on the eighth day after birth is a fitting reminder that "children of promise" come not from man's flesh (works), but from God's faithfulness. Flesh has no part in the covenant. Flesh must be cut away because in Kingdom matters "flesh is hostile toward" and unable/unwilling to submit itself to the work of God's Spirit.[13] Just as God reduced the size of Gideon's army until the odds of victory were impossible, so he cut away Abraham's flesh from the very point at which natural life-seed flows.

God's message was clear: *You cannot produce a child yourself. Not by might nor by the power of your flesh, but by My Spirit will My promise be accomplished.*[14] Regardless of how sincere or religiously motivated, any effort or work we try to add on our own "in the flesh cannot please God."[15] When God fulfills His promises, He doesn't want anyone tempted to think it was done by their "own power."[16]

Notice the sequence of events. Abraham received and believed the promise before he was circumcised. Therefore, circumcision is the sign of God's promises, not His commands. Circumcision was not a badge of merit or morality, but "a seal of the righteousness of faith."[17] Abraham became "the father of all who believe without being circumcised, that righteousness might be credited to them."[18]

## Living by Faith

Once again we see that faith-in-God's-promise—not faith-plus-adequate-effort to be good—saves us. In Chapter 8, I will explain "faith without works" because I am not telling you that being saved by grace means you can become lawless and do any wicked thing your heart desires. That's the challenge with this subject—it has so many interconnecting parts and passages. Please stick with me point by point, and I hope to answer all your questions before you finish reading.

> **Circumcision is the sign of God's promises, not His commands.**

"Faith alone" is troubling to religiously minded people. The *Spirit of the Pharisee* inspires fear in the Church by predicting that without explicit and exacting standards for behavior, Christians everywhere will live hedonistic lives. They will pervert liberty into license. That notion is neither true nor biblical. Go back to the Bible record: In the two thousand years after God's command to Adam, the closest thing we see to a moral code was God's injunction to Abraham, "Walk before Me, and be blameless (whole, complete, with integrity)."[19]

Abraham and his descendants, Isaac and Jacob, lived in the Promised Land prior to (i.e. without) the Law. They didn't have a list of behavior-prescribing guidelines from God—except don't murder and don't eat meat with blood.[20] The *people-of-promise* lived not by rules but by promises:

> By faith [Abraham] lived as an alien in the land of promise, as in a foreign land, dwelling in tents with Isaac and Jacob, fellow heirs of the same promise . . .      —Hebrews 11:9

In God's Master Plan to redeem our race, circumcision is a reminder of God's promise to credit righteousness by faith, not by works of our flesh, and by that faith to become children of Abraham. As Paul says, "It is not the children of the flesh who are children of God, but the children of the promise are regarded as descendants."[21] We trace our spiritual ancestry all the way back to Abraham, the "Father of Faith," not just as far back as Moses, the "Giver of the Law."

## 'Chosen' Not 'Obedient' Ones

Those who suggest that we are saved by faith *and* obedience, by promise *and* commands, cannot find any suitable biblical characters to match their formula. No one was obedient enough to qualify. In fact, one of the most encouraging elements of the Bible is its refusal to sugar-coat things. The Bible certainly isn't a collection of stories about super-saints. Our spiritual ancestors lived flawed lives.

Just as most readers forget about Noah's drunken escapade after the Flood, so most believers skip too quickly over the details of Abraham's life after he offered Isaac on the altar and after Sarah died. Did you know that Abraham "took another wife, whose name was Keturah,"[22] and that she bore him six additional children? The circumcised Father of faith conceived children who had absolutely no part in God's promise; Abraham sired a child of faith (Isaac) and, subsequently, children of flesh. One of his offspring was Midian, whose descendants later opposed, deceived, and enlisted occult powers against the people-of-promise.

**The Bible certainly isn't a collecton of stories about super-saints. Our spiritual ancestors lived flawed lives.**

And in addition to a new, younger wife, Abraham also took concubines who bore sons. He sent some of those boys away "to the land of the east" (i.e. out of the Promised Land) after paying them off and cutting them out of his will.[23] That's not exactly Sunday School material.

Abraham didn't lose the righteousness he gained by faith just because he slipped into less-than-righteous behavior. His later activities were unwise and unspiritual, to be sure, but they did not jeopardize his acceptability to God— or his place as our ancestor of faith. I'm not arguing for legalized prostitution or polygamy. I'm simply pointing out that Jesus' ancestors had very uneven track records. What set them apart was not their sinlessness, but their faith.

> **God's people are the chosen ones, not necessarily the obedient ones.**

If we read the biblical record thoroughly and dispassionately, it's clear that biblical faith heroes cannot pass for behavior role models.

As the years rolled on, God reinforced His simple message: righteousness in the fallen world is based not on people's behavior, but on His promises. For instance, the twins born to Isaac and Rebekah were both "descendants" of Abraham, yet God favored Jacob over Esau—but certainly not "because of [Jacob's] works."[24] Jacob was a conniving, unrighteous man who exploited circumstances for his own benefit. He stole his brother's birthright and blessing. Nevertheless, "though the twins were not yet born and had not done anything good or bad,"[25] God chose Jacob to receive His promise of blessing.

God's people are the chosen ones, not necessarily the obedient ones.

The Old Testament continually communicates the theme of human failure. But overriding human waywardness stands a grander message: God's unending, affectionate graciousness toward prone-to-wander people—His mercy matching, stride for stride, every errant step they take. That is what God is like. The key to our family connection with God is not obedience to His commands, but faith in His promises. We do not gain relationship with God through obedience, nor do we lose that relationship through disobedience.

God's people are people of promise.

## Reasonable Sins

Many of the fears that plague us about the power our sin might have to disqualify us from God's mercy are the result of thought patterns we might not even realize we have. So, if I may, I would like to shift our discussion from Bible passages to the corridors of our minds to highlight the mental gymnastics we go through in our guilt and shame.

As silly as it sounds, most of us believe that God tolerates a reasonable number of trespasses in our life—as long as they are not too numerous or extreme. For normal, everyday sins, it's fairly easy to believe we are saved by grace. It might not be a conscious thought, but we presume His grace provides sufficient forgiveness for us as long as we don't blow it too badly. *After all, we're human . . .*

As a result, we subconsciously evaluate the frequency and the magnitude of our wrongdoing. If it is only occasional, or if it's been a long time since we last fell short (in that particular manner), we count our trespass as a *reasonable* failure. It isn't difficult to believe God forgives such things because we don't do them that often. *Everyone slips up once in awhile,* we say to ourselves.

We also gauge the severity of our sin. Like Olympic diving judges, we judge between really awful and appalling behavior at one end of the scale, and things we *probably* shouldn't have said or done on the other end. The more shocked we are that we did it, the higher its score. We don't agonize over small infractions because we presume God forgives low-scoring sins. *Nobody is perfect . . .*

But big sins—the habitual or horrifying ones—are a big deal. That's why our soul has a fleshy plan to help God with His promise if our sins seem too numerous or too monstrous for Him to easily forgive. If we worry that our failure is becoming too frequent, we promise never, ever to do it again. In our odd way of thinking, a promise to ourselves and to God renders the sin less severe—

> **Our soul has a fleshy plan to help God with His promise if our sins seem too numerous or too monstrous.**

and more easily forgiven. Of course, if we continue to blow it, we are forced to find new ways to really, really, sincerely and truly promise . . .

Likewise, if our failure is shockingly bad, and even we cannot justify or excuse what we did, our soul offers a subtle escape. We consider, *Is my sin less terrible than others' sins?* If so, our crazy logic assures us that God can (and will) forgive us. It wasn't that bad, after all. We would never come out and say so, but our thought is wickedly reassuring: *If I'm not as bad as others, I'm not too bad for God.* It's why we think things like, *At least I didn't do (fill in the blank)* . . .

## Uh-Oh

Notice, however, that in both cases, *we* judge our own behavior and decide how reasonable our sin may be. Using the measure of our sin to excuse it actually backfires on us, and establishes a horrific possibility that ever-threatens us with the unspeakable: If we embrace the idea that God forgives a *reasonable* number or magnitude of sin, then one day (*was it yesterday?*) we might cross over the limit.

Think for a moment about the feelings of guilt and self-reproach that hang on and weigh you down. Despite knowing doctrinally that you are forgiven, the sense of disqualification and probation remains. Probe those feelings a bit further, and you will likely discover that it isn't the fact of your guilt that troubles you. What unsettles you are the possible implications of your guilt:

- "Is there a fixed number of times God will forgive me for a particular wrongdoing?"
- "If I *consciously* plot out my sin, does grace cover it with forgiveness in the same way that grace covers my unintentional sins?"
- "Can I step so far away from the path of obedience that I lose my footing on sin's cliff face, and forever fall from grace?"

Just to be sure we never do take such a fall, we promise to redraw personal boundaries. We offer sacrifices, vows, and penance as proof that we have learned our lesson ("for the last time"). Being the one who broke things so badly, it's so tempting (and noble-feeling) to be the one who promises to fix them. Promising God what you will do, instead of relying on what He has promised to do, turns you into the promise-maker, and you unintentionally edge God out of His role as Promise-Maker.

Uh-oh.

## Falling Away

The Enemy of our soul capitalizes on the fear that our sinfulness will cause us to "fall away" from God. The early Church faced the same temptation. Many believers, especially among the Jews, were "running well"[26] and "standing firm,"[27] "waiting for the hope of righteousness" by faith.[28] But "false brethren" snuck in "to spy out" the "liberty" they had in Christ Jesus, "in order to bring [them] into bondage."[29] In perhaps the strongest caution given to believers in all the New Testament, Paul warns,

> You have been severed from Christ, you who are seeking to be justified by the law; you have fallen from grace. —Galatians 5:4

Wow. What could be more frightening than to be "severed from Christ" and to have "fallen from grace"? What did Paul mean by that expression? At first glance, it seems to confirm our worst fears. But that is because the Church today uses the expression "fallen from grace" synonymously with "fallen into sin." We call believers (especially leaders) "fallen" when it becomes publicly known that they committed big, obvious sins (usually of either the sexual or financial variety).

But is that what Paul meant? In this passage, he doesn't mention a huge sin

**"Falling from grace" is buying into the lie that closeness to God is secured by either (1) the smallness/infrequency of our sin, or (2) the sufficiency of our sacrifice.**

committed by the Galatians. Instead, he connects their *fall from grace* to "seeking to be justified by the Law." Instead of justification by faith, they chose justification by the Law—they no longer relied on God's work of grace. That's why Paul says they had "fallen from grace." Their trust was not in Christ's obedience and sacrifice, but in their own. "Falling from grace" is buying into the lie that closeness to God is secured by either (1) the smallness/infrequency of our sin, or (2) the sufficiency of our sacrifice (i.e., penance, remorse, and promises about future behavior), plus an adequate level of future obedience.

## Falling Away from Promise

The terrible danger for believers is not falling into sin (we're already there), but falling away from total reliance on what Christ already did for us.[30] The expression "fallen away" is used in another passage, and because of inexact Bible study, some in the Church use "fallen" to describe people whose sins seem too awful to be easily covered by God's grace:

> For in the case of those who have once been enlightened and have tasted of the heavenly gift and have been made partakers of the Holy Spirit, and have tasted the good word of God and the powers of the age to come, and *then have fallen away*, it is impossible to renew them again to repentance . . . —Hebrews 6:4-6

We're not certain who wrote this Book in the Bible, but the author confronts the legalistic heresy in his day—and in ours. The *Spirit of the Pharisee* teaches that grace has limits, and if you do too much evil (in quantity or quality), you can exhaust the supply of grace. The writer acknowledges that some who "tasted the good word of God" have "fallen away,"[31] but he doesn't say exactly how or why. Many readers today assume it was because they sinned grossly and relentlessly without remorse. However, when we place this quote in context with the whole letter, another explanation for their "fallen" state seems more likely.

Just prior to this passage, the writer encourages believers to "press on to maturity" by moving beyond basic truths in the Kingdom, such as "repentance from dead works" and (instead) "faith toward God."[32] Subconsciously, you probably associate repentance exclusively with bad behavior and gross sin. However, in this case those long-ago believers were being reminded that relying on grace meant not relying on their own moral accomplishments and righteous deeds. The writer urged them to repent of their trust in the works of the Law because "the Law made nothing perfect."[33]

Once we experience the all-sufficiency of grace and Christ's gift, and then fall back into the belief that we earn salvation through good works, it's almost impossible to change back (i.e., repent). "Falling away" is not synonymous with sinning grossly, but with abandoning the "Sabbath rest" provided by Jesus—and trusting in our own works, instead.[34]

The entire Book of Hebrews repeatedly warns against the temptation to stop believing in God's promises—and turn back to the "weakness and uselessness" of the Law which makes "nothing perfect."[35] "Take care," Hebrews cautions, "Lest there should be in any one of you an evil, unbelieving heart, in falling away from the living God."[36]

People who fall away, "who shrink back to destruction," are those who stop living by faith alone "to the preserving of the soul."[37] In Paul's words, such people try to create "a righteousness of [their] own derived from the Law," instead of "the righteousness, which comes from God on the basis of faith."[38]

The *Spirit of the Pharisee* bullies us with fear. It twists the words ("falling away") and intimidates us with eternal consequences. Its threat is plain: "If you do not maintain more righteous behavior, you will 'fall away' and lose the salvation God provided for you." What could be more

**Legalism tempts us to discard God's grace for our own works.**

precarious than trying to (re)establish righteousness by perfect obedience to rules—by exerting our flesh? *Legalism* tempts us to discard God's grace for our own works. It wants us to make the same mistake Abraham and Sarah made, so we give birth to Ishmael, not Isaac.

Just as Paul cautions the Galatians, the writer of Hebrews explains that the "fallen" are not those who have fallen into sin, but those who have fallen from complete reliance on grace. The great danger for believers is to "neglect so great a salvation" and "drift away" from resting in what Jesus did for us.[39] Unbelief holds more peril than disobedience.

There is a good reason why we call ourselves *believers* not *obeyers*. God provides through promise, and we receive what He promises solely with faith. When we try to "help" God with our own salvation, we unintentionally "neglect so great a salvation."[40] Scripturally, the bigger danger to our eternity is not bad behavior, but any good behavior we use to establish our own righteousness.

Believers who fall away from faith in God's promises are no longer believers.

## True Confidence

Grace is our only true "confidence"—and the only hope for eternal reward.[41] Though the apostle Paul was exceptionally qualified to have confidence in the Law, he realized how flimsy that standing was before God. He understood "true circumcision," gloried in Christ Jesus, and "put no confidence in the flesh."[42] He was like a climber who refuses to put any of his weight on a loose rock he knows is certain to dislodge from its place and tumble down the mountainside. Instead of relying on the Law to hold him up, Paul placed all his weight on the Rock that never gives way.[43]

It isn't easy to keep relying on Jesus' completed work. That's why Peter urges us, "prepare your minds for action, keep sober in spirit, fix your hope completely on the grace to be brought to you at the revelation of Jesus Christ."[44] People who use obedience to the Law as either the means for or the proof of their justification unintentionally abandon grace. They substitute their promises for God's. They might not realize what they are doing, but their supposed repentance is not prompted by the Holy Spirit, but by the *Spirit of the Pharisee*.

Could it be that you find no satisfying answer from God when you plead for the forgiveness He has already granted in Christ because your penitence actually sounds something like this:

> God, I can't rely exclusively on Your promise to forgive me. I'd like to do something, too. I have not been able to keep Your commandments to me, but I'm sure I will be able to keep my promises to You. So, put Your trust in my promise to be good from now on . . .

How much confidence do you put in your ability to be good? When depressive and heavy guiltiness drives you to self-reproach and tries to convince you that God gives up on you and your ministry, could much of your worried guilt and reproachful regret be a hint that you are *making* promises rather than *believing* them—and putting your weight on the wrong rock?

---

[1] 1 Corinthians 10:11
[2] 1 Peter 1:10-12
[3] Titus 1:2; (See also Luke 1:68-77; Romans 1:2; 3:21; 16:25-26)
[4] Luke 1:70
[5] Hebrews 11:6
[6] Hebrews 11:1-2
[7] Hebrews 11:4
[8] Hebrews 11:5
[9] Hebrews 11:7
[10] Genesis 6:9
[11] Romans 4:13
[12] Genesis 17:10
[13] Romans 8:6-7
[14] See Zechariah 4:6
[15] Romans 8:8
[16] Judges 7:2
[17] Romans 4:11
[18] Romans 4:11
[19] Genesis 17:1
[20] Genesis 9:4, 6
[21] Romans 9:8

22  Genesis 25:1
23  Genesis 25:6
24  Romans 9:11-12
25  Romans 9:11
26  Galatians 5:7
27  Galatians 5:1
28  Galatians 5:5
29  Galatians 2:4
30  Philippians 3:3-4; Hebrews 3:6; 4:16; 10:19-21, 35; 1 Peter 1:13; 1 John 3:3
31  Hebrews 6:5-6
32  Hebrews 6:1
33  Hebrews 7:19
34  Hebrews 4:11
35  Hebrews 7:18-19
36  Hebrews 3:12
37  Hebrews 10:39
38  Philippians 3:9
39  Hebrews 2:1, 3
40  Hebrews 2:3
41  Hebrews 10:35
42  Philippians 3:3
43  Matthew 7:24ff
44  1 Peter 1:13

# Chapter 7

# A Deliverer and a Law-Giver

At the foot of the Acropolis is a restaurant where pastor George insists we eat every time I come to Athens. Nestled beneath pine trees, in full view of the ancient ruins, and just a four-minute walk from where Paul stood at Mars Hill, it's the perfect place to have lunch and enjoy a coffee. Even with lots of tourists around, the ancient setting creates a mood of stillness and reflection, and in the midst of such an obvious span of time from long-ago to today, most current problems find perspective.

After the previous night's lecture, I felt the need for conversation. Perhaps my insecurities prompted me to open my heart, but I really wanted to know from George if the truth I was sharing was making sense to anyone. I knew he would be kind but straightforward. As I drank my after-lunch latte, I blurted out, "It's tricky, you know—how believers see the Law and struggle with Grace."

He nodded knowingly, stirred his cappuccino, and invited me with his eyes to continue. Perhaps he knew I needed to confess. I was giving a lecture that made it seem as though I no longer struggle with the ambiguities of the Law and Grace—and my own battles with guilt feelings. The *Spirit of the Pharisee* continues to whisper to me. I still have a hard time finding the dividing line between godly remorse and ungodly self-reproach.

"Honestly," I said to George, "it's difficult to let go of the semi-security the Law offers to us. The Pharisees' misguided perspective about the Law at least gives us a chance to throw our sincere effort into the equation. Initially, we try hard to be good, and when we're disobedient, we can still work hard (at being good) by being really disgusted with our disobedience.

> **I still have a hard time finding the dividing line between godly remorse and ungodly self-reproach.**

"When I fail to do right, I have a chance to redeem myself by feeling terrible about what I've done. In a convoluted logic, the catechism of the *Spirit of the Pharisee* provides a way for me to feel somewhat good when I've been bad—by reproaching myself. Make sense?"

George is a man of few words, but he assured me he understood—and that I was helping his congregation. "I would like," he said, "if you would visit us twice a year to teach. I observe you are a man who ministers in friendship. You walk among us. We believe you because you do not present yourself above the people, but among them."

I understood he was telling me that my transparent struggle with all this stuff lent a weight to my teaching that made it helpful—precisely because I struggled with this for so long. The ragged-edged guilt and despair that tore through my heart when I failed never felt quite right, and it certainly didn't match up with what I knew about God. I knew something was not right, but I didn't know how to put a finger on it.

His words—and an afternoon nap to fight the jetlag—invigorated me for the next night of lecture. I definitely needed the extra boost because the mood of the audience was growing slightly impatient. I think even Angela, my translator, was worried I was never going to get around to answering people's simple questions: *Why does guiltiness continue to consume me even though Jesus has forgiven me? How can God use me after I've messed up so badly?*

## A Deliverer

I resumed the timeline of the Old Testament, leaping forward more than 400 years after Abraham received the covenant promises. I asked for a show of hands from everyone who had seen the movie, "The Ten Commandments." Like all Hollywood adaptations, its fanciful plot inserts characters and twists of events not found in the Bible, and leaves out many that actually are there.

But the movie holds true to the Bible record in the manner in which God rescued infant Moses from Pharaoh's death-edict for all newborn Jewish boys. While at the river bathing, Pharaoh's daughter spied the basket carrying baby Moses. Delighted by the infant, she adopted him and, thereby, for the next 40 years exposed Moses to all the education and training of the ruling world-order. He tasted Egypt's passing pleasures, and became well acquainted with its power. The best Egypt had to offer was his for the taking.[1]

Obviously, Moses was Jewish, not Egyptian. It's the whole point around which the early plot turns. In the movie, Prince Moses was a grown man when the old crone of a nurse showed him the swaddling cloth with Hebrew design that was in the basket when Pharaoh's daughter found him. That was how the director of *The Ten Commandments*, Cecil B. DeMille, artfully sidestepped the fact that Moses realized he was a Jew while still a young boy. He was circumcised! And all the other boys he knew were not.

One day Moses witnessed an Egyptian taskmaster beating one of the Hebrew slaves. Moses tried to rescue his countryman, but ended up killing the Egyptian. He quickly buried the body in a shallow grave. The next day, Moses saw two of his true countrymen fighting each other. When he came to the aid of the one being picked on, the aggressor in the quarrel taunted Moses, inquiring, "Are you going to kill me like you killed the Egyptian yesterday?"

Moses knew the word was out. So, he fled Egypt into exile in Midian, where he lived as a shepherd for the next 40 years with his wife, Zipporah. That was a far cry from the courts of Egypt, and a long way from the people he sought to free from tyranny. Nevertheless, God heard the cry of His enslaved children, and "remembered His covenant with Abraham, Isaac, and Jacob."[2]

Four decades after Moses tried to do the job on his own, God recruited him as a deliverer: "Come now, and I will send you to Pharaoh, so that you may bring My people, the sons of Israel, out of Egypt."[3]

> **Four decades after Moses tried to do the job on his own, God recruited Moses as a deliverer.**

Predictably (since he is our ancestor, and like us), Moses hedged. No one wants to directly refuse God, especially after He has just spoken from a burning-but-not-consumed bush. But Moses didn't relish the thought of returning to a country where he was a wanted criminal. *After all*, Moses thought to himself, *I already attempted a rescue once, and failed.*

So, Moses replied, "Who am I, that I should go to Pharaoh, and bring the sons of Israel out of Egypt?[4] I have no credentials or credibility, no training and no skills of diplomacy." He was probably also thinking, *You've got to be kidding?! How do You expect one man to succeed against the most powerful nation on the earth?*

"Tell them 'I AM' sent you!" God answered.

**Signs and Wonders**

Still unconvinced, Moses inquired what to do if the Name alone didn't persuade people to listen. In reply, God demonstrated the "signs and wonders" that would attend Moses' message.[5] He turned Moses' staff into a snake and back again into a staff; his hand turned leprous as snow, and then became like new. Moses had no way of knowing that God was establishing a timeless pattern in His relationship with our race. Forever after, God signaled and effected deliverance among His people with "signs and wonders."[6] They are the trademarks of deliverers sent by God that testify "to the word of His grace."[7]

Thousands of years later, the writer of Hebrews references this pattern of proof—God's signature on a message of grace. Jesus the Deliverer, like Moses, came to an obstinate people, offering them "so great a salvation."[8] He confirmed His appointment by God, and His message from God, "by signs and wonders and by various miracles and by gifts of the Holy Spirit."[9] The Apostle Peter appealed for his countrymen to believe that just as He promised He would, God provided another Deliverer like Moses: "Jesus the Nazarene, a man attested to [them] by God with miracles and wonders and signs which God performed through Him,"[10] in order to deliver them from "the agony of death."[11]

## "Bridegroom of Blood"

Now back to our story. Convinced of God's power, Moses still doubted his own suitability for the job. He presumed God needed a capable, qualified spokesperson. Being "slow of speech and thick of tongue (and a stutterer),"[12] Moses wasn't much of a speaker. God told him plainly, "I will be your mouth, and teach you what to say."[13]

Most of us know that story fairly well. But just after the burning bush episode, Moses and God have another conversation, and that story is one of the most unusual in the entire Bible. It is the pivotal episode in Moses' life. Moses agreed to deliver God's message to Pharaoh and began his journey back to Egypt. Along the way, however, God confronted Moses and sought "to put him to death."[14]

God was profoundly displeased with Moses. But why would God try to kill the very person He just commissioned to ministry? God could not have been upset

**But why would God try to kill the very person He just commissioned to ministry?**

about Moses' lack of worthiness because his spotty resumé and meager job skills had already been vetted. Was this just a whimsical God changing

His mind and keeping His servants guessing at His next moves? Moses wasn't rebelling; he was doing God's will.

Or was he?

Was Moses violating something of such a critical nature that God was willing to suspend His deliverance efforts for His people, in order to maintain His covenant with them? Was the basis for their salvation from Egypt so crucial, so critically essential that God would risk allowing them to remain in captivity until He could send them an appropriate deliverer?

**The rescue rested not on Moses' competence but on God's covenant.**

Let's review what we know.

Moses tried to deliver the slaves with his own strength and resourcefulness. He failed. With all the natural giftings and prerogatives of earthly power as a prince of Egypt, he could not deliver God's people. Just as it had been impossible for Abraham to father a son-of-promise in his own strength, so it was impossible for Moses to deliver people from Egypt in his own power. God did not choose Moses for his personal prowess. He was not impressed by Moses' skill as a guerilla fighter or orator. Moses' giftings, training, calling, or strength were never the point.

God didn't need a deliverer acting in his own strength. The rescue rested not on Moses' competence, but on God's covenant. That covenant explains why God confronted Moses. Though circumcised himself, Moses forgot to maintain the sign of the covenant within his own family. Moses had not circumcised his son. As we learned, the covenant was based on God's promise, not His commands. That meant his descendants would be disqualified from the covenant blessing:[15] righteousness by faith not flesh.

Moses the (eventual) Law-giver betrays his character by having his wife do the cutting with a flint knife. Was he too squeamish or too proud or too embarrassed to perform the act himself? Who knows. But after Zipporah finishes circumcising their son, she throws the severed piece of flesh at Moses' feet, and shouts, "You are a bridegroom of blood to me,"[16] and leaves him to return with the boys to her father's house. Again, not exactly Sunday School material.

Few preachers I know make a Sunday sermon out of that story—and the detail that when Moses conducted his deliverance ministry in Egypt, he and his wife were separated.

Perhaps Moses' failure to circumcise his son was unintentional, but God would not allow Moses to obtain deliverance for people by his own strength and fleshly ability. God is single-minded about offering salvation and deliverance solely through the faith-covenant. Salvation (deliverance) comes only by means of faith;[17] it is an act of grace—something God does for His people-of-promise, not something they manage to do for themselves.

Long before God gave the Law of commandments to Moses, He reinforced the covenant of faith in the Law-giver's life. God stands opposed to any suggestion that fleshly works—however well-intentioned or sincere—can accomplish salvation. He would not allow Moses to be an instrument of rescue until Moses truly understood the faith-covenant between God and the descendants of Abraham. The Law of commands inscribed on stone tablets did *nothing* to alter the law of faith that secured God's covenant with His people.

## God of Deliverances

The God of Abraham, Isaac and Jacob, the "Lord of All,"[18] is never idle in working salvation for His people,[19] nor is He slow about His promises.[20] He is not the god described by deists, who made the world like a watch, and then sits by letting it run on its own. No, the God who loves us and gave the life of His Son to redeem the world is a "God of deliverances"![21] He is not an aloof, disinterested Evaluator who simply imposes penalties on offending parties like an anonymous, back-office clerk who knows nothing about—and cares nothing for—the individual people.

He seeks and saves those who are lost.[22] "God our Savior" doesn't want anyone to perish,[23] but God cannot simply ignore or excuse sin, because it has the power to destroy everything He creates. Let me be abundantly clear about this point: God's love and grace do not eliminate the certainty of our sin. They do not magically do away with right and wrong. Though grace saves us from the eternal consequences of a guilty verdict, it does not alter reality and pretend we never sinned. Every sin has some kind of consequences.

**Sin maneuvers us toward unbelief; repentance turns us back around.**

Sin hardens our heart. That is dangerous because our heart is our belief organ; we believe in our heart—and confess with our lips.[24] When someone's behavior is continually out of sync with God's word and way, that disconnect can creep into the person's heart. Disobedience increases the level of disbelief.

We do not lose our salvation as a result of something we do (or don't do). But the longer we live in ungodly patterns—especially if we do wrong over and over without remorse, regret, or repentance—ungodly patterns worm their way into our heart and begin leading us away from our faith. In Chapter 8 we will talk more about people who intentionally "forsake the right way" and go astray, but those people are not the same as those of us who sincerely want to walk the "right way" but sometimes fail.[25]

Sin maneuvers us toward unbelief; repentance turns us back around. Some of the regret and grief you feel after you have sinned is good and appropriate—and prompted by the Holy Spirit.[26] It is a sign of repentance, and an acknowledgement that you have been headed in the wrong direction. Your sorrow over what you have done draws you back to Jesus.

**Judge and Advocate**

God is completely for us, but completely against our sin.

He is both our Advocate and our Judge. Given His dual role in Creation, how could God remain just and righteous while rescuing a sinful people? No individual human can grasp the enormity or complexity of

God's position. If we were tried under the Law of Moses, we could only be found guilty. The verdict was inescapable. Under that Law, a just Judge could not possibly find us innocent of all charges. He would need to pervert justice to declare us "not guilty." So, what did God do?

To answer that simple question, I must once again opt for a long answer—but you will likely see my point even before I finish explaining it. What we call the Old Covenant is actually newer than what we refer to as the New Covenant. Confusing, huh? The covenant God made with Abraham predates the covenant He set up with Moses. Faith came before the Law as the means of righteousness. The New Covenant is really the older covenant like John speaks of the new-but-old commandment to love one another;[27] it just wasn't completely explained until Messiah came.

God alone is the "Law-giver,"[28] so He has the prerogative and power to create laws and jurisdictions. Because the "Law of Moses" is usually referred to simply as "the Law," we forget it was not the only or oldest Law. Perhaps it will help if we distinguish the two sets of laws by giving them characterizing names. I'll call one the *law of belief,* introduced into the world through Abraham; the other, introduced through Moses, I'll refer to as the *law of behavior.* Scripturally, what I'm calling the *law of believing* is variously

**God didn't change the justness of His character in order to find us innocent; He simply changed the "law" under which we were tried.**

named as "the law of faith,"[29] "the law of the Spirit of life in Christ Jesus,"[30] "the law of Christ,"[31] and "the law of liberty."[32] Another name for the *law of behavior* is "the law of physical requirement."[33]

God didn't change the justness of His character in order to find us innocent; nor did He change the facts in our cases. He simply changed the "law" under which we were tried. He chose to try our case under the "law of faith,"[34] "apart from works of the Law,"[35] so that "He might be just and the justifier of the one who has faith in Jesus."[36]

Because God exists outside the limits of time, it is always a bit nonsensical to pin down precise moments in human history when God takes action. But within our understanding of time's passage, we can say that from the moment Adam and Eve disobeyed in Eden, God counteracted the influence of the *sin-force* by establishing a "law" by which people could be justified.

**The presumptuous prophet in Athens wanted me to pronounce judgment on a people who were already justified.**

Under the *law of belief*, we were justified. To *justify* means to *declare innocent or righteous*. God justifies us, and certifies/authorizes our righteousness. Who can argue with God? Once He makes a judicial ruling, who can "turn it back?"[37] When God converts people's eternal status from unrighteous to righteous, no argument or finger-pointing by man can overrule His official declaration. The Apostle Paul exclaims, "Who will bring a charge against God's elect? God is the one who justifies; who is the one who condemns?"[38]

The presumptuous prophet in Athens wanted me to pronounce judgment on a people who were already justified. He wanted me to reinstate the temporary jurisdiction of the *law of behavior*,[39] under which he and I would both be condemned!

Besides, contrary to the angry prophet's pronouncement, God doesn't judge anyone, "but He has given all judgment to the Son."[40] Jesus, who paid the price for our justification, now sits beside God, interceding for us. Can you see the vivid contrast between Jesus' loving intercession and the fuming condemnation inspired by the *Spirit of the Pharisee*? God abounds in mercy, and He restores life to people "because of His great love with which He loved us—even when we were dead in our transgressions."[41] The false prophet's frenzied demand for judgment was unbiblical and nonsensical. "God did not send the Son into the world to judge the world."[42]

**No Judgment?**

A loud silence stole from the audience onto the stage where Angela and I stood that night in Athens. Just as I could sense their skepticism, I can almost hear the objections being voiced in some reader's minds: "*Don't our sins matter? Isn't that what people call 'cheap grace' and a 'license to sin?' Can we really just do whatever we want—without any consequence? Are you claiming that God's love eliminates judgment, and in the end offers eternity to humanity without regard to their faith in Christ or their sin?!*"

Generally speaking, heresy in the Church can almost always be identified by what it says about (1) who Jesus is; (2) what He accomplished on the Cross; and, (3) God's judgment of people. Most deep error betrays itself with unorthodox, unscriptural perspectives about these three doctrines. I am fully aware of heresies trying to worm their way into Jesus' Church, but I do not want to address one off-base teaching (*license*) with another (*legalism*).

I'm not telling you God is too loving to judge or punish. I am not saying everyone goes to Heaven—or that universal reconciliation is God's ultimate objective. The Church has been entrusted with the "ministry of reconciliation," but the Bible is clear that the only option for reconciliation between God and us is through Christ.[43] God wants everyone to be saved—to become part of the escaped remnant;[44] nevertheless, only those who believe in and accept the atonement provided by Jesus on the Cross will enjoy eternity with God.

That's the whole point—those who believe!


## The Judgment Day

You might ask, "*What about the Judgment Day, when people will be 'judged according to their deeds'?*"[45] OK, let's answer your question with more Bible study. The Judgment Day is pictured most fully in the Book of Revelation,[46] near the very end. The Bible does, indeed, say that humanity will be judged "according to their deeds," apparently from a record of their life tallied in a ledger.

But most people don't realize that two books are described in that scene: one contains the journal-account of our lives; the other, called the "Book of Life (of the Lamb),"[47] simply registers the names of believers in

Christ. Picture the two books in your mind's eye. One catalogs each of your life-deeds; the other simply lists your name—if you have confessed Jesus as Savior.[48]

**God doesn't grade on a curve.**

From a human perspective, there are many "good" people living "good" lives. What about all the good people in the world? It seems fairer to us if God stacked up all of our good deeds on one pan of the cosmic balance and weighed them against our nasty thoughts and misdeeds on the opposite pan. Contrary to what some teachers espouse, that actually offers no hope for anyone. Every single human being comes up short in such a tit-for-tat assessment.

God doesn't grade on a curve.

All of us are fatally fouled both by original sin and by our own wrong-doing. Regardless of our moral codes, life philosophies, belief in a Supreme Being, good or bad intentions, religious background, failures or accomplishments, we fall hopelessly "short of the glory of God," and our only hope for redemption is God's grace-gift "in Christ Jesus."[49] That reality explains the concluding verse in the Bible's description of the Final Judgment. It is the verse almost no one remembers in their vague recollections of the Judgment Day:

> And if anyone's name was not found written in the book of life, he was thrown into the lake of fire.     —Revelation 20:15

Our deeds cannot save us; they have already damned us! Jesus said, "Everyone who confesses Me before men, I will also confess him before My Father";[50] and "I will not erase his name from the book of life."[51] That is why Jesus' love gives us such "confidence in the Day of Judgment."[52] The book of life records the names of those found innocent under the *law of belief.*

For the legalist, our name in that book seems too easy, too accommodating and convenient—as though it doesn't matter what we do (wrong), as long as we believe. But turn that argument around and you will see things from God's perspective. He is desperate to save you. He knows it doesn't matter what you do (right), you will never be able to do right enough to be declared righteous. So, after shutting "everyone under sin,"[53] and declaring us universally "disobedient" under the *law of behavior*,"[54] He tries us under a different law, the *law of belief*.

## Courtroom Advice

Picture a guilty murderer facing trial. He cannot deny the clear evidence against him, so his defense strategy is to offer character witnesses who vouch for his *good* character—despite the occasional lapses. He may have a temper, but murder isn't *really* part of who he is. He tries to further his case by contrasting himself to other "really evil people like Hitler." The Judge still pronounces him guilty—and sentences him accordingly.

Another equally guilty man elects not to compare himself to other offenders; neither does he offer character witnesses to convince the court that he isn't what his misdeeds seem to indicate he is. Instead, he relies on a remarkable plea-bargaining that his Attorney says is allowed in the Court of Heaven. The man's court-appointed Advocate urges him, "Confess your guilt, throw yourself on the mercy of the Court. I will speak to the Judge in chambers on your behalf! Believe Me when I tell you this is the only way to avoid life in prison!"

> So, after declaring us universally "disobedient" under the *law of behavior*, He tries us under a different law, the *law of belief*.

Trusting the counsel of his Attorney, the guilty man confesses before the Judge—then remains silent. He accepts the simple truth that no matter how strenuously he argues details in his case, he will be found guilty. After a short recess, the Judge returns from His chambers, and ends the

We have been found righteous under the *law of belief*, and we will not be tried again under the *law of behavior.*

proceedings by mysteriously declaring the court satisfied in full. No one—except the defendant and his Advocate—can believe their ears. The prosecutor is left standing, sputtering in protest, "But the evidence, the evidence . . ."

Jesus explains the dual nature of final judgment by saying, "He who hears My word, and believes Him who sent Me, has eternal life, and does not come into judgment [under the *law of behavior*]."[55] We pass "out of death into life," and never go on trial again for the decisive verdict on our life. We have been found righteous under the *law of belief,* and we will not be tried again under the *law of behavior.*[56]

God "justifies the ungodly," reckoning their faith as righteousness,[57] so it all comes down to a simple question: Will you trust the words of your court-appointed Advocate—or not?

---

[1] Acts 7:22
[2] Exodus 2:24
[3] Exodus 3:10
[4] Exodus 3:11
[5] Exodus 4:9, 17; Deuteronomy 26:8; Nehemiah 9:10
[6] Daniel 6:27
[7] Acts 14:3
[8] Hebrews 2:3
[9] Hebrews 2:4
[10] Acts 2:22
[11] Acts 2:24
[12] Exodus 4:10
[13] Exodus 4:12
[14] Exodus 4:24
[15] Genesis 17:14
[16] Exodus 4:25
[17] 2 Timothy 3:15; 1 Peter 1:9
[18] Acts 10:36; Romans 10:12
[19] Deuteronomy 32:47; Philippians 2:13

20  2 Peter 3:9
21  Psalm 68:20
22  Luke 19:10
23  1 Timothy 2:3-4
24  Romans 10:9
25  2 Peter 2:15, 20-21
26  John 16:6
27  1 John 2:7-8
28  James 4:12
29  Romans 3:27
30  Romans 8:2
31  1 Corinthians 9:21
32  James 1:25; 2:12
33  Hebrews 7:16
34  Romans 3:27
35  Romans 3:28
36  Romans 3:26
37  Isaiah 14:27
38  Romans 8:33-34
39  See Luke 16:16
40  John 5:22
41  Ephesians 2:4-5
42  John 3:17
43  Acts 4:12; 2 Corinthians 5:18-19
44  1 Timothy 2:4
45  Revelation 20:12-13
46  Revelation 20:11-15
47  Revelation 13:8
48  Philippians 4:3; Revelation 22:19
49  Romans 3:23-24
50  Luke 12:8
51  Revelation 3:5
52  1 John 4:17
53  Galatians 3:22
54  Romans 11:32
55  John 5:24
56  John 3:18
57  Romans 4:5

# Chapter 8

# "Faith Without Works"

Mistaken impressions are part of life. Kids, for instance, think something terrible is being done to them when forced to eat mushrooms or asparagus. It isn't until later in life they discover how wrong they were. Piano lessons that prevent youngsters from more time with friends or the computer eventually allow those young musicians to be part of the church worship band. At the moment of application, no discipline seems like a good thing—even though it sets up a better future.[1]

In the spiritual dimension, we misunderstand a great deal. That's why God expressly tells us He doesn't think the way we do.[2] Jesus began most of His mind-blowing statements with the preamble *"Verily, verily . . ."* because His words didn't make much sense to the ways of the world. In fact, He warned people that if they wanted to follow Him, they would need to "deny" themselves.[3] A better translation reads *"contradict" their usual way of thinking.* Kingdom truth is often counter-intuitive to natural

> **Our feelings of hopeless dread and death-dealing guiltiness are profoundly off the mark from what God wanted for us.**

reasoning: the last end up first; those who willingly lose their life gain it; and servants become leaders.

An underlying premise in this book is that our feelings of hopeless dread and death-dealing guiltiness are profoundly off the mark from what God wanted for us when He sacrificed His Son. A good and merciful God wants to extend goodness and mercy.[4] I know the counter-argument: God hates sin, so the agonizing doubts about our standing with Him after our misdeeds are simply the result of our misbehavior. We're being convicted of our sin—and sickened by it—so we won't commit our wrongs again.

But something still doesn't add up.

If it is always and only the Holy Spirit working righteousness into my soul (i.e. sanctifying me), why are His marvelous trademarks sometimes so absent in the process? Where is the "love, joy, peace, patience, kindness, and goodness" that I usually experience as a result of His touch?[5] The consequence of sin is death.[6] I accept that. For years I assumed that suffocation by grief for my guilt was my "death." The *all-is-lost* worry, the *too-late-you-fool* self-reproach, and the multiple repetitions of "I'm sorry God" were just part of living out "death" for my sin.

But deep down I knew God isn't like that.

He paid an incredible ransom to get me released from judgment. Jesus is faithful to forgive and cleanse me from every stain. Most of the time, I find welcome and kind mercy when I return/repent. I feel sheepish and slightly embarrassed, and I definitely regret what I have done. Curiously, though, I have new hope for my future because I'm back with the One who has the plans. He's like the father of the prodigal son, and I feel His joy over my return. He is my Advocate, not my adversary, and He embraces me so tightly that nothing can worm its way between me and His love. That is what God is like.

The suffocating self-loathing, the foreboding sense of judgment felt more like what I would expect from the prodigal son's older brother. The evil-spirited, and our own misunderstandings, cloud that truth about God and His joy over the return of His wayward children.

Like my audience in Athens, are you beginning to realize there may be several interrelated answers to the question: *Why do I still feel guilty if I am truly forgiven?*

In this chapter I want to look at some specific misunderstandings that create much of the fearful guilt plaguing you. Believe it or not, some of your confusion and torment is the result of misinterpreting a couple of words that get used frequently without much biblical definition: *judgment* and *works*.

## Now and Future Judgment

Let's face it, for us judgment is a harsh, merciless-sounding concept. We associate judgment with wrath, damnation, punishment, and cruelty. Judgmental people condemn and look down their noses at others, right? Critical, fault-finding, disapproving, rejecting—these are our synonyms for judging. Because we have such negative impressions, it's hard to wrap our minds around a biblical picture of judgment.

> **The goal of God's judgment is to unlock people's chains, not to imprison them in shackles.**

I've been saying this in the last few chapters: God's judgment is primarily a tool of deliverance. And the goal of God's judgment goal is to unlock people's chains, not to imprison them in shackles.[7] He uses it to set His children free from who/what dominates them, so they have relief from their afflictions.[8] Take, for instance, the Judges who governed Israel after Moses and Joshua. Deborah, Gideon, and others fought against Israel's oppressors in order to deliver God's people from consequences of earlier sins.[9]

Likewise, God is a "judge for the widows."[10] He is on their side and advocates in their favor. Messiah (Christ Himself) judges with spiritual perception and principles "for [the sake of] the afflicted," to overturn life's unfairness.[11] Read closely, and you will see that, most of the time, God's judgment is explicitly on behalf of people like us—not against us. Judgment steps in between us and the things that try to dominate us.

Unfortunately, when we superimpose a fear-filled, negative picture of judgment, we lose sight of God as our Champion who intervenes as a Savior.[12] He takes hold of shield, spear, and battle-axe to "contend with" and "fight against" our oppressors, and He rises up in judgment to meet those who "pursue" us.[13] God's judgment delivers and defends us from any evil—whether that evil lurks around or within us. He breaks the links between us and what He condemns; His judgment cuts away the sins that would otherwise carry us away.

To fully explore biblical judgment would require a whole book, but for our purposes, I'm simply asking you to reconsider the possibility that judgment is a tool God uses for good. The next time you read a story of judgment in your Bible, ask yourself, *What good is being preserved? Who is being delivered or defended? What change-for-the-future is being accomplished, so that, in the end, God's people are better off?* If you look for that good, you will see it.

## Side-by-Side Realities

Misjudging judgment as an essentially negative thing isn't our only mistake. We also tend to lump all judgments and their consequences—in this life and the next—together. God doesn't. In His eyes, the correction and chastening His people need while they are maturing on earth is entirely different from the ultimate judgment He will render looking back on their entire life. Judgment works differently in our life *now* than it does in *eternity*.

Judgment in our lives on earth keeps us moving forward on track—even when we come up short in our efforts to live as God wants us to live. We don't always "walk in a manner worthy" of our calling.[14] We're supposed to mature,[15] and "grow in respect to salvation,"[16] until our thought patterns, behavior, attitudes, and perspectives become like the Lord's. But God doesn't have an angry or disgusted desire just to "straighten us out." Instead, He is developing us, so we more fully live out His life before others.

God's judgment in our present life is like parenting: Correcting our kids' attitudes isn't the same as cutting them out of our will. We discipline them, but we don't disown them. We give them incentives and admonitions to obey; we censure and dicipline when they disobey. The whole point of such guidance is to get them into their future—well tooled, well trained, and well situated.

> **God's judgment in our present life is like parenting: Correcting our kids' attitudes isn't the same as cutting them out of our will.**

Just as I wanted to teach each of my children to drive a car, God wants to teach you and me how to live life spiritually. His intention is far grander than just teaching us how to drive according to the rules; He's most interested in helping us go places and do things that are not possible without learning to function well in the spiritual world.

God is "good and ready to forgive."[17] Though ultimately forgiving, He still disciplines, reproves, and corrects the children in whom He delights.[18] God was an avenger (punisher) of Israel's misbehavior.[19] He wanted better for His people, so He judged and cut off wrong beliefs and practices that would hinder them from reaching what He promised to them. As I explained before, our natural thinking separates judgment from mercy— as though they are mutually exclusive and opposite concepts. That makes it hard to understand how God meets our sins with both mercy *and* judgment, in order to secure our future.

God sees our failures eons before we commit them. Nevertheless, despite our future foul-ups, we are already "called children of God,"[20] and we have been "sealed" with the Holy Spirit as a down payment on our eternity.[21] We have "eternal life,"[22] and we do "not come into judgment, but [have] passed out of death into life." He disciplines us with *earthly* consequences because we are His legitimate offspring,[23] and He nullifies *eternal* consequences for exactly the same reason.

Think of yourself as the captain of a storm-damaged, off-course ship that is listing badly in high seas. If another vessel approached, offering to "right" your tilted boat, and give you a portable GPS navigation device to find your way to port, would you judge that captain an evil seaman or a good Samaritan? While it is true that God judges the sin in your life, declaring you are off-course and sinking, He doesn't offer such "righting" and course-correction as a warning that He plans to sink your ship if it ever again lists or drifts off-course.

God's *earthly* judgment corrects us, "so we become more like Him."[24] It expresses His love, not His wrath. It is developing us, not damning us.

## Faith without Works

We don't need "Holy Hubert" or an angry Athens prophet to raise the question we puzzle over ourselves: *How can faith and sin coexist in my life?* Every honest believer knows this side-by-side reality: our faith and our failures. Failed and forgiven. We wonder how long the cycle can continue before God wearies of the pathetic joke. What hypocrites we are. Adding to the doubt about the legitimacy of our faith, we recall the statement, "Faith without works is dead."[25]

*That's me*, we conclude. *I believe in Jesus, but maybe my belief isn't enough to save me since I'm not very good at being very good.*

According to the Book of James, true faith—faith with enough power to save—expresses what it believes by doing things. Faith unaccompanied by works is "useless,"[26] lifeless and unengaged like an unemployed laborer. Genuine faith leads to "works," but what sort of "works" accompany true faith? That is the crux of the question.

> The *Spirit of the Pharisee* misleads us to presume that *faith-with-works* is the same as *faith-without-(too much)-sin.*

The *Spirit of the Pharisee* introduces a subtle misunderstanding that blurs our Bible study and misleads us to presume that *faith-with-works* is the same as *faith-without-(too much)-sin.* The two are NOT the same. What keeps many believers in dread under the *law of behavior*, instead of in hope under the *law of belief,* is the faulty notion that *faith-with-works* is the same as *commands-with-obedience.*

Demons "believe [in God] and shudder,"[27] but their belief, according to James, is not true faith. Full faith believes in God and in His promises. The *evil-spirited* believe in God, but they neither receive nor believe promises from Him. They do not (cannot) act on His promises. James contrasts the uselessness of demons' belief in God's existence with Abraham's and Rahab's belief in God's promises. Demons do nothing to act upon their belief. Abraham and Rahab do. Look closely, though, at what Abraham and Rahab do to live out their faith. They acted on promises, not commands.

Abraham was "justified by works when he offered up Isaac his son on the altar."[28] Abraham was willing to sacrifice the very child God promised because he believed *Jehovah-Jireh* (the God Who Provides) would keep His promise some other way.[29] Abraham placed his son on the altar because he believed in God's promise to make him the Father of many nations. His faith had "works." Pause for a moment to consider Abraham's behavior if God had not asked him to act on a promise. Stripped of spiritual promise, the sacrifice of his son would be premeditated infanticide—an immoral act expressly forbidden by any standard of righteousness!

Rahab, likewise, did things that corresponded to her belief in a promise. She was "justified by works when she received the messengers and sent them out by another way."[30] She bet her life on God's faithfulness, and acted out what she believed by aligning herself with His people in order to share their future. Her faith had "works."

**True faith acts on and responds to God's promises.**

In like manner, Noah built an ark under blue skies,[31] Joshua felled Jericho's walls by walking in circles,[32] Gideon reduced the size of his army before battle,[33] Daniel spent the night among lions,[34] etc. Samson, David, and others mentioned in the Hall of Faith in Hebrews 11[35] "gained approval through their [works of] faith,"[36] not by living a perfect life, free from deeds of the flesh and wayward actions. True faith acts on and responds to God's promises. Faith that does not act on the basis of God's promise cannot save anyone—in any situation.[37]

## Questionable Works

I wonder what the angry prophet in Athens would say about Abraham in his waning years when the Father of faith sired all those children of flesh with several different women?[38] Or about the brothel owner, Rahab, who was "justified" by lying to city officials,[39] hiding two enemies of her people, and striking a bargain for her life?[40] What was her culminating "work of faith"? She "tied a cord of scarlet thread in the window" through which she let the spies down.

Not exactly a noteworthy moral accomplishment.

Her belief in a promise—not a command—prompted her to act. The spies promised her, "Our life for yours if you do not tell this business of ours."[41] Nowhere in the bargain did it stipulate that she quit her line of business. Several days, at least, passed before Israel besieged Jericho, and one more week before the walls fell. Was Rahab still working during those days? Did her establishment remain open for business? Who knows? In either case, "Rahab the harlot" (ever wonder why that is her enduring name?) passed along her business profits to her son, Boaz, who later married Ruth, the mother of Obed, the grandfather of King David.

> The fear legalists introduce is that no matter what you believe, if you do not behave well enough, your faith cannot save you.

When legalists remind you and me that "faith without works is dead," they imply that such works are ethical accomplishments, rule-keeping, and reasonably good behavior. They are actually saying/ implying that faith without an acceptable level of morality is not bona fide faith. The fear they introduce in your thought is that no matter what you believe, if you do not behave well enough, your faith cannot save you.

*Works of faith* are not synonymous with *works of Law*. *Works of faith* are responses to promises, not commands. They are a consequence of putting our trust for the future in God's hands; they are not successful attempts to always align our behaviors with God's commands. Which commands did Abraham or Rahab obey? What Law or point of morality were they following by their "works" highlighted in the Book of James? Quite simply, none.

The *Spirit of the Pharisee* accuses us of denying our faith every time we sin. It plants the threatening thought in our minds, *If Christ truly was your Savior, you wouldn't continue to commit sin.*

What a lie. The fact that we need a savior makes us unacceptable to Christ our Savior? Our perpetual need for forgiveness proves that we shouldn't receive it? Our failure to live perfectly renders us undeserving of grace?

That is heresy, the doctrine of a demon.

Believers sin; we all sin. Only liars claim otherwise.[42] So, *works of faith* cannot possibly be interpreted as a sinless existence. The true work of faith is believing in Christ (see John 6:28-29). Despite wrong choices we make, we choose to believe Jesus' death and resurrection cleanses us from sin, and transforms us into new creations in God.[43]

**The level of our obedience to the Law of Moses is never the basis upon which our relationship with God hangs.**

Our *work of faith* is like that of the guilty man in my illustration from the previous chapter. Because we have complete trust in our "Advocate with the Father, Jesus Christ the righteous," we confess our guilt, offer no self-defense, and let Him, who "makes atonement for our sins,"[44] speak with the Judge in chambers. When threatened with eternity in prison, we perform our *work of faith*: we confess our sin, confess Christ—and let Him confess us before God.[45]

That is Gospel, the doctrine of a Savior.

Will we disappoint ourselves and do things Jesus doesn't want us to do? Yes. But once saved by grace, we also have fresh desire to follow the precepts of God written in our hearts. We care about being obedient because we care about God. We do not deny His claim on our lives,[46] or His call to holiness.[47] We know we were "bought with a price," and we want to glorify God in our bodies.[48] We just don't always succeed.

The deeper our faith, the more deeply God's word and Spirit plumb the reaches of our psyche to realign the patterns of our heart and mind with His.[49] Our belief begins a sanctifying, cleansing work in our lives from the inside out. Faith in and love for Jesus motivate us toward increased obedience, but the level of our obedience to the Law of Moses is never the basis upon which our relationship with God hangs.

Because we prefer easy-to-repeat phrases and simple black and white propositions, it's hard to express the full implications of grace without sounding heretical—especially to legalistically influenced believers. I understand their concern because many "voices" are urging the Church to abandon Truth in order to be more relevant to society. Just as the Scriptures prophesied, some teachers have "gone astray from the truth,"[50] denying the necessity of personal salvation through the Cross of Jesus Christ.

As I reminded my Greek friends, only if we die with Christ, will we live with Him; only if we endure in faith will we reign with Him in heaven;[51] only those who "confess with [their] mouth Jesus as Lord, and believe in [their] heart that God raised Him from the dead, will be saved; for with the heart a person believes, resulting in righteousness, and with the mouth he confesses, resulting in salvation."[52]

The Truth hangs in the balance between two lies about our eternity and our relationship with God. On one side, liars tell you, *"You don't have sin—at least, none that really matters; God loves you despite whatever imperfections you might have, and in the end, all will be fine. Don't worry; be happy and try not to get into too much trouble."*

On the other side, liars tell you, *"You don't have faith—at least, not enough to save you; your imperfections are too large and too long-lasting, and in the end, all is lost. Worry; be grieved and realize you are already in too much trouble."*

## The Faith Covenant

There is another misconception that causes you to labor with worrying feelings of condemnation and eternal insecurity. Many believers inaccurately imagine that the Old Covenant arranged for salvation-by-obedience, and the New Covenant altered that offer with salvation-by-faith. God never offered two parallel paths to salvation—one of *Grace* and the other of *Law*. He never intended to save people by their obedience to the *law of behavior*; its purpose (discussed more fully in the next chapter) was to remind people of their sin—and the need for forgiveness.[53]

During the twenty-four hundred years before Moses brought the stone tablets down from the mountain, as well as in the years before Christ died on the Cross, God vindicated both the circumcised and the uncircumcised, the godly and the ungodly, under the *law of belief* through faith credited as righteousness.[54]

The commands in the Old and New Covenants are essentially the same. In the Old Covenant, God wrote His Law on stone tablets[55] for "the seed of Abraham."[56] In the New Covenant, God inscribes His Law on heart tablets for the seed of Christ.[57] We no longer obey an external standard of rules and regulations. Instead, God prompts us toward the right things to do—and away from the wrong things—through the inner witness of His Spirit. As He promised, He puts His righteous commands into the very places of decision-making in our life.[58]

> **Grace doesn't remove sin from the world—just from our trial before the Eternity Court.**

God's grace does not annul His commands. Sin is still sin. Jesus explained, "Until heaven and earth pass away, not the smallest letter or stroke shall pass from the Law until all is accomplished."[59] The New Covenant does not erase the commands, just the record of our disobedience to those commands. Grace doesn't remove sin from the world—just from our trial before the Eternity Court.

The key provision of the *faith-covenant* is that sin lost its authority to determine our eternal destiny. Why? Because God declares us free of sin—by faith "apart from works of the Law."[60] Sin is no longer our master,[61] and it cannot carry us away to judgment like withered leaves driven before a furious wind.[62] The wind still blows in our life—sometimes as strongly as it did before we lived "by faith in the Son of God."[63] Now, however, we "abide" in Him like fresh leaves attached to a fruitful vine.[64] No blast of sinful wind can pluck us from the "Branch of the Lord,"[65] Jesus Christ.[66]

## Nailed to the Tree

Paul paints a vivid picture for his friends in Colossae to explain this great miracle. God as Judge declared the "certificate of debt" (the evidence of our wrongdoing) inadmissible in our trial; in fact, He Himself took an additional step to make sure that "hostile" list of damning accusations will never find its way into the Eternity Court: He "nailed it to the cross."[67] No evidence of our wrong-doing will ever be found.

Sins we commit over the course of our life do, I suppose, get added to the record of violations. I know for certain that my list grows ever longer. But no power in the universe will ever pry loose the spikes with which that ever-lengthening register was hammered to the Cross. It may grow longer, but it's never coming off the Cross to condemn me. Through "His own blood" Jesus obtained eternal redemption for me.[68]

**What terrifies us is the fear that our sins have the power to break Jesus' faith-covenant with us.**

That makes Him the mediator of a New Covenant.[69] "Therefore," Paul tells us, "Let no one act as your judge."[70] False prophets are especially intimidating when they breathe threats of judgment against sincere believers who are only too aware of their failures and shortcomings. It's an old ploy—but one that works quite effectively because our sins stare us down daily. We don't need a prophet to harp on our shortcomings. Like King David centuries ago, we pray,

"Wash me thoroughly from my iniquity and cleanse me from my sin. For I know my transgressions, and my sin is ever before me."[71]

We're not really afraid of admitting our sins; we've already confessed them to Jesus. What terrifies us—and what these false prophets prey upon—is the fear that our sins might have the power to break Jesus' faith-covenant with us.

They *do not*. They never will have such authority.

As I taught this precious truth in the seminar that week in Greece, the room went suddenly still. No one moved. A deep, wide silence opened around us, and I could feel my friends groping for permission to believe. Like wanderers too long beneath the desert sun, they couldn't decide if my words were true drink or cruel mirage. Even my translator, Angela, didn't know where to look as we stood there in the silence.

That's when, without notes or prompting, I began to quote aloud, "If we say that we have no sin, we are deceiving ourselves and the truth is not in us. If we confess our sins, He is faithful and righteous to forgive us our sins and to cleanse us from all unrighteousness."[72]

Somehow, I knew to punctuate that promise with another: "For I am convinced that neither death, nor life, nor angels, nor principalities, nor things present, nor things to come, nor powers, nor height, nor depth, nor any other created thing, will be able to separate us from the love of God, which is in Christ Jesus our Lord."[73]

---

[1] Hebrews 12:11
[2] Isaiah 55:8
[3] Mark 8:34
[4] Exodus 33:18-19; Psalm 23:6, 27:12-14. 65:3-6
[5] Galatians 5:22
[6] Romans 6:23
[7] Psalm 107-10; 146-7; Isaiah 61:1
[8] Psalm 34:19
[9] Genesis 15:14
[10] Psalm 68:5
[11] Isaiah 11:3-4
[12] Isaiah 19:20; Jeremiah 20:11

13 Psalm 35:1-3
14 Ephesians 4:1
15 See 1 Corinthians 13:11; Philippians 3:12-14; Hebrews 5:12-14
16 1 Peter 2:2
17 Psalm 86:5
18 Hebrews 12:5-6
19 Psalm 99:8
20 1 John 3:1
21 Ephesians 1:13
22 John 5:24
23 Hebrews 12:7-8
24 Hebrews 12:9
25 James 2:20
26 James 2:14ff
27 James 2:19
28 James 2:21
29 Genesis 22:12-14
30 James 2:25
31 Hebrews 11:7
32 Hebrews 11:30
33 Judges 7:1ff; Hebrews 11:34
34 Daniel 6:16-20, 27; Hebrews 11:33
35 Hebrews 11
36 Hebrews 11:39
37 James 2:14; see also Matthew 11:1-2, 6
38 Genesis 25:1-6
39 James 2:25
40 Joshua 2:1ff
41 Joshua 2:14
42 1 John 1:8
43 2 Corinthians 5:15-17; Galatians 6:15
44 1 John 2:1-2
45 Matthew 10:32
46 1 Corinthians 6:19; Galatians 3:28-29, 5-24
47 2 Corinthians 7:1; Ephesians 1:4; 4:24; 1 Peter 1:15
48 1 Corinthians 6:20
49 Hebrews 4:12
50 2 Timothy 2:18
51 2 Timothy 2:11-12
52 Romans 10:9-10
53 Hebrews 10:3
54 Romans 29-30, 4:6-13
55 Exodus 31:18; Deuteronomy 4:13
56 Galatians 3:16
57 2 Corinthians 3:3

58 Jeremiah 31:33
59 Matthew 5:18
60 Romans 3:28
61 Romans 6:14
62 Isaiah 64:6
63 Galatians 2:20
64 John 15:1-6
65 Isaiah 11:1; 60:21; Jeremiah 33:15; Zechariah 3:8
66 Romans 8:33-39
67 Colossians 2:14
68 Hebrews 9:12
69 Hebrews 9:15
70 Colossians 2:16
71 Psalm 51:2-3
72 1 John 1:8-9
73 Romans 8:38-39

# Chapter 9

# Why the Law?

I wish I could have arranged for the sound of a hammer pounding slowly and steadily to grow louder and louder as the Greek audience sat silently before the tea break. But I hope you will always remember the rhythmic sound of your sins being nailed to the Cross. When doubt assails you and when wicked but religious-sounding whispers suggest Jesus' work is not quite enough to cover your sin, let the cadence of Calvary drown it out. It is not the sound of a gavel pounding out your guilt; but the echo of the hammer that nailed Jesus—and your debt certificate—to the Tree.

After all the preliminary and background information I've presented, it's time to answer at least one of your specific questions: Why did God give the Law of Moses, especially after so many centuries?

God gave the Law of Moses to us for several reasons—all of them good. In fact, the only way to discover why God speaks or acts is to look for the benefit He aims to give to the world. God is good and only does good.[1] He sends rain on the righteous and the unrighteous,[2] and He continues to guide people even after they transgress the Law.[3] So, let's start there. God's Law was intended for our good. It was designed to better our life, not beggar it.

> **God's Law was designed to better our life, not beggar it.**

The Law is not an about-face, a change in character by "I AM," the changeless One.[4] The God who mapped lands of promise for His people is the same God who gave them the Law. The Promise-Giver is also the Law-Giver. Life would go better for His children if they obeyed His Law.[5] By following its counsel, they would "possess the good land,"[6] drive out their enemies,[7] and live longer.[8]

Instead of seeing the Law as one of many gracious gifts from a kind and good Father, most believers view the Law as an act of frustration and disfavor, written when God lost His temper and spelled out the justifiable reasons for His rage. Nothing could be further from the truth, but that misconception, like propaganda, slants the facts and writes off all the evidence of God's boundless love. It sets believers on the wrong trajectory for understanding how the Law and Grace work together, and turns the Law into a cruel cudgel. God did not write His Law on tablets to bash the world; He wrote it to benefit us. If God loves the world enough to give His Son as a ransom for all,[9] how can we imagine that He gave His Law with another heart?

> **If God loves the world enough to give His Son, how can we imagine that He gave His Law with another heart?**

Dear reader, I must warn you: My ultimate goal is to show you what a false hope the Law is for your spiritual security and development. But before I destroy your confidence in the Law, I want to convince you how good it is—and what God's kind love intended to accomplish with it.

So, what were some of the benefits God gave to the world twenty-four hundred years after Adam and Eve sinned in the Garden?

### #1—A Counter-Balance to Evil

The Law protected humanity from being overwhelmed by the *sin-force*. God used the Law to restrain an unchecked tide of evil from completely engulfing humanity. There were two trees in the Garden of Eden: the "tree of the knowledge of good and evil" and the "tree of life."[10] After Adam and Eve ate of the tree of knowledge of good and evil, God banished them from the Garden to ensure they did not eat of the other. In His mercy, God did not want fallen man to live forever.

Six-year-olds don't have a refined repertoire of evil. What youngsters do under sin's influence is a far cry from what sixteen-year-olds or thirty-six-year-olds do. If they lived centuries instead of decades, imagine how skilled-in-evil people would become: wickedness, greed, envy, murder, strife, deceit, malice, slander, insolence, arrogance, lovelessness, and mercilessness would all but overwhelm us.[11]

> **The Law enhanced humanity's immune system to resist the *sin-force* infection.**

At the root of the ruin, the *sin-force* bent humanity toward evil. The Law helped bend our race back toward its original design by providing an offsetting power. It enhanced humanity's immune system to resist the *sin-force* infection.[12] If you imagine a set of balancing scales like those used in olden times to weigh out equal measures of precious metals, you'll have a good idea what I'm talking about. When the *sin-force* first entered our world, its heavy weight crashed one side of the scales to the table.

The Law didn't rebalance the scales completely, but it significantly offset the weight of evil. Without the Law, our world would now be overwhelmed by unspeakable wickedness—and be unbearable to all but the most depraved.

The Law could be compared to a spiritual edging-stitch that God sewed back into the fabric of Creation to keep it from fraying. The Law could not prevent holes worn in the cloth, but it did keep the God-intended patterns of Creation from completely unraveling.

*Legalism*, the false religion spread by the *Spirit of the Pharisee*, only emphasizes one purpose for the boundaries in the Law: They are borders you and I must not cross—or God will punish us. Certainly, we suffer a measure of spiritual death every time we cross boundaries to participate in evil. But the Law was made for man, not vice-versa, and the primary purpose for borders was to protect us from moving into the domain of evil. Yes, God wanted check points to inhibit people from crossing into evil, but He also wanted to prevent evil from invading our world unchecked.

**The Law was made for man, not vice-versa, and the primary purpose for borders was to protect us from moving into the domain of evil.**

"In the beginning" God inscribed a "boundary of light and darkness."[13] Following the Flood, He issued an "eternal decree" setting the sand as "boundary for the sea" to prevent the waters from (again) covering the earth.[14] Just so, He drew His Law as another "line in the sand" to keep evil at bay. Though tsunami seas sometimes flood ashore, the ocean will never again utterly bury the earth. Evil sometimes crosses its borders, too, but never as much as it would if unrestrained by God's Law.

### #2—An Identity Marker

THE LAW DISTINGUISHED GOD'S PEOPLE FROM ALL OTHERS. Because He gave the Law to His children of promise, not to every nation, the Law identified God's people as *His* people. The One who gathered the outcasts of Israel and healed the brokenhearted among them, also declared statutes and ordinances to them—not to "any [other] nation."[15] God signified His intimate association with Israel by "setting before" them the "whole Law,"[16] just as a man presents his fiancé with an engagement ring.

Israel's Heavenly Father gave the Law so things would go well for His children, and they would live long in the land.[17] Though God could have selected any people of the world to be His, He chose Israel.[18] He differentiated Israel from other nations in several ways: He fought for them to assure their inheritance; He "redeemed" them and "made a name for Himself" by doing "awesome things" against their oppressors;[19] and, He entrusted them with His "oracles."[20]

When our children were growing up, we likewise had several family rules. We wanted the kids to be successful, so we put limits on their behavior and guidelines on their attitudes. Exactly like birthday parties, new clothes, and meals, the rules expressed love for *our* children, and helped our kids establish patterns for life. But no matter how poorly our children kept the rules, their relationship with us was never in jeopardy.

Abraham's descendants were already God's own possession, literally His "special treasure."[21] His Law was not the starting point for their relationship. God's people walked in obedience and disobedience; they possessed and forfeited their inheritance in regular, almost predictable cycles. Nevertheless, they remained His people throughout their wayward history. Neither their identity nor their relationship with God was in question when He gave them the Ten Commandments and the Law.

True, lawbreakers who persisted in their evil were eventually cut off from Israel, but that happened primarily when people's sinfulness threatened to pervert the way of God for the whole nation. Don't forget what I explained earlier in Chapter 8: in order to protect your eternity, God will judge and remove wayward thoughts and impulses in your life. Just as Paul delivered a man's physical body over to destruction, "so that his spirit [would] be saved in the day of the Lord Jesus,"[22] so God will cut off lawlessness in our hearts or minds. But He does that because of our relationship with Him—not to qualify us for relationship with Him.[23]

The *Spirit of the Pharisee* whispers fearful accusations that insinuate God is reconsidering His role as our Father because we have broken the rules. Legalistic thoughts keep us in a state of perpetual probation. They threaten us with our obvious failures, and point out how close we are to losing it all: *One or two more goofs and God will be finished with you. You need to work harder, be better, and do more to regain His favor.*

## #3—A Profitable Guide

THE LAW TAUGHT PEOPLE HOW TO LIVE BOUNTIFULLY. God's Law gave His people extraordinary insights into life. As Maker of heaven and earth,[24] God knew precisely how life was supposed to work. The original "good" that He poured into Creation still existed, but it was horribly polluted. The world was like a stagnant pool of brackish water. God offered His Law as a filtration device to strain out the impurities and contaminants infecting the water. He didn't want His children getting sick from what was in the world-water.

"His statutes and His commandments" were given to benefit the descendants of Abraham.[25] If His people were "careful to do all His commandments" (i.e., follow His instructions), they would be greatly advantaged "above all the nations of the earth," and "blessings [would] come upon and overtake" them wherever they went.[26] He shared His "way of life" so His people would get the most blessing and the least trauma in the no-longer-right world.

> **God offered His Law as a filtration device to strain out the impurities and contaminants infecting the water.**

Aren't we all trying to find our way in life? Don't we want to follow a life course of happiness and well-being? The Law helped people find and walk in God's ways. Perhaps you have noticed how frequently the Bible refers to "ways"—the ways of God and ways of the world. For example, David eagerly sought to know God's ways of "salvation" when faced with his sin.[27] David wanted to be led in God's truth because his own paths led him into death. There is a way that makes sense to our natural, sin-clouded mind, but that way usually cuts us off from life as God designed it.[28]

In fact, the ways of God, manifested in His Law, were intended to produce such attractive results in the lives of His children that other people would want to get in on those benefits. God's plan was for other nations to stream to the house of God,[29] and come to Israel's light because of the advantage His Law obviously gave them.[30] The nations would envy God's wise and understanding people who had such amazing patterns for life,[31] and they would say, "Let us seek the Giver of such advantage that 'He may teach us about His ways'."[32]

It's ridiculous to imagine that people would be attracted to a grim, austere code of ethics that drained joy and satisfaction from life. That could not be

God's plan for winning the hearts of the world. *Legalism* turns the ways of God into punishing gauntlets instead of promising paths. Everything becomes a threat against us, and the only reward for obedience that *legalism* holds out to us is merely that we will avoid punishment. It shrinks the meaning of "good" from a bountiful state of being that God wants for us, to a meager comment on behavior God expects from us.

## #4—A Clear Inventory

THE LAW PROVIDED A DETAILED REGISTER OF SINS. God gave the Law to point out "lawless and rebellious" deeds,[33] and to fortify humankind's conscience so that it could better distinguish right from wrong. Though people's conscience warned them when they headed in a wrong direction prior to the Law, no one knew when they actually arrived at an explicitly wrong place. It was difficult to distinguish between being "tempted by evil" and giving "birth to sin."[34] Being tempted toward a sinful act isn't exactly the same as committing the sin. We know there is a difference. Jesus was tempted, but He never sinned.[35]

**Legalism turns the ways of God into punishing gauntlets instead of promising paths.**

God augmented people's vague sense of direction (conscience) with a clear list of destinations-to-avoid. Right and wrong were no longer relative to people's circumstances. The Law brought an absolute ethic to the world, much like a landmark on the horizon provides a constant reference point with which to evaluate where people went in their hearts and minds.

Prior to the Law, exact instances of sin could not be "imputed" or charged to anyone.[36] The Law was "added because of transgressions,"[37] meaning its purpose was to identify and itemize sinful activities. By enumerating individual sins, it increased everyone's awareness of their personal sins.[38] How could people recognize their sins without a specific list of sinful activities? They would not know, for instance, that coveting is sin "if the Law had not said, 'You shall not covet.'"[39] The Law convinced people that they were sinners.

It may surprise you to realize that God gave His Law primarily for those who wanted to get life right—not those determined to do it wrong. Before the Law was given, people wanting to live right had no precise knowledge of how far off track they had wandered; now we know in great detail when, where, and how we go off-course.

But the detailed knowledge of right turns and wrong turns provided by the Law never guaranteed people would always choose the right path. It was a set of instructions for individual drivers, not an autopilot device. All of us are "flesh, sold into bondage to sin,"[40] and the flesh-side of our being constantly tries to jerk our steering wheel in the wrong direction.

> **Legalism contends that knowing right from wrong should be enough for people to resist temptation.**

*Legalism* contends that knowing right from wrong should be enough for people to resist temptation. That's why one of the most-repeated phrases in its twisted catechism condemns sinful but sincere believers like us by saying, "*You should have known better.*" Indeed, we did; we do. Because we knew exactly what we were doing and lurched into sin anyway, we have no answer for *legalism's* accusation. Self-reproach floods our soul. Subtly, the *Spirit of the Pharisee* shifts our disgust away from our sin and on to us. People bound by *legalism* come to hate themselves as much as, if not more than, they hate their sin.

## #5—A Universal Verdict

THE LAW PRONOUNCED EVERYONE GUILTY. The Law leveled the playing field, making Law-breakers of all. It expanded everyone's awareness of wrong in their lives.[41] That's what the Bible means when it says, "The Law came in so that the transgression would increase."[42] The Law didn't cause people to sin more; rather, its decrees testified against each person, so no one escaped a guilty verdict.

Some sins tempt us more than others. No matter what wrongs we avoid doing, if we violate even one command, we become "guilty of all."[43] Though we might not covet, the dishonor we show our parents still makes us Law breakers. The Law "shut up everyone under sin,"[44] and confined everyone in the same prison cell, wearing the same prison-issue jumpsuit. Each inmate may be guilty of different offenses, but each one is (equally) guilty. Some in prison might be model prisoners, but they are still guilty.

The hundreds of statutes and ordinances in the Law make it incredibly frustrating, don't they? It is so detailed, so extensive. Why are there so many commands? Think of the Law as a giant fishing net. A net with more strands and a tighter weave catches more fish. God wants to "catch" even the smallest sins, so no one escapes the judgment of the Law. Jesus made the Law more impossible to keep when He explained that a sin in our heart makes us as guilty as the person who physically commits the wrong we confined to our thoughts.[45]

I can understand why you might be feeling a bit betrayed by what you are reading. You hoped this book would remove your feelings of guilt and shame. Yet, I'm telling you that universal guilt is a good thing—one of the benefits of the Law. I know that's not very uplifting, but in a sense, what you're feeling makes my point.

Let me explain.

Just as a compass always points north, so the *Spirit of the Pharisee* shamefully aims your attention perpetually at your wrong-doing. The center-point of *legalism* is your guilt. No matter how you turn or maneuver the compass, the needle continues to disgrace you by adamantly pointing back to your guilt. *Legalism* hones in on and targets your guilt like a heat-seeking rocket. Whatever you try to do with your guilt or wherever you try to hide it, *legalism* sniffs it out.

> **Whatever you try to do with your guilt or wherever you try to hide it, *legalism* sniffs it out.**

*Legalism* and the Law are *not* synonymous.

True, the Law convinces us of our guilt. But why? Like a friend who points out a smudge of dirt on our cheek, the Law tells us frankly of our wrongs so we can remove the uncleanness. The central theme of the Law is to keep God's people "separated from their uncleanness . . . so that they will not die in their uncleanness"[46] The commands in the Law of Moses do root out and find our guilt, just like we sift through the soil in a garden to find—and remove—weeds. God wants your guilt out and gone; *legalism*, on the other hand, never wants you separated from your guilt. It wants you so interwoven with your guiltiness that you lose all hope your sins can ever be taken away.

Doesn't all our guiltiness drive us to one consuming question: "What can take away my sin?" Oh, yes. And that critical question leads us to the most overlooked benefit of the Law.

## #6—A Precedent for Atonement

THE LAW INTRODUCED SACRIFICE FOR SIN. Of all the advantages the Law gave to humanity, the foremost is also the most easily forgotten—or never noticed. It's a classic case of not being able to see the forest because of all the trees.

> **As much as the Law identifies sin, it also points to the possibility of atonement.**

Most people, believers included, have the impression that the Law consists primarily of regulations and rules— things we are supposed to do or not do. We view it as a set of commands and consequences, prescribed behaviors and punishments. Tragically, our overall impression of the Law is quite lopsided, weighted mostly toward penalties visited on disobedient people like us. We skip over and hardly remember any of the blessing and bounty promised by the Law in a broken world.[47]

Even more amazingly, we miss its main point: The Law is more about forgiveness than about guilt.

The Law is very black and white. Good and bad. Holy and profane. But as much as the Law identifies sin, it also points to the possibility of atonement—and the way to receive forgiveness. For every act of unrighteousness and each violated precept, God lists meticulous instructions for sacrificial redemption. It's so simple, really. The Law is a blueprint for redemption.

Let me give you an example of how we misread the Law. Consider the Book of Leviticus. As the least narrative of the Books of the Law, it's not most believers' favorite read. Most of us know it as the book that slowed or halted our earnest resolution to read through the entire Bible in one year. Genesis and Exodus are easy reads compared to Leviticus. Though it doesn't include the Ten Commandments (found in Exodus and Deuteronomy), even casual Bible readers know that Leviticus contains many specific rules, commandments, and requirements that we call the Law.

I admit that I have not actually counted up the verses, but if you divide the total number of verses in Leviticus into two categories—one labeled *statutes* and the other *sacrifices*—one list will far outnumber the other. There are many 'thou shalt' and 'thou shalt not' verses, but in passage after passage, God's Law details the means and methods of atonement, cleansing, and redemption when God's people fail to follow His words.

Read it yourself—the first six chapters of Leviticus describe the "laws" of sacrifice, burnt offerings, grain offerings, peace (with God) offerings, sin offerings, and guilt offerings. All these "laws" are for the sake of people who have violated the Law. They are rules for reconciliation after the point of failure.

**The Law establishes patterns of atonement, and it points us toward forgiveness again and again.**

True, the Law minces no words; it is straightforward and unequivocal about guilt. There isn't supposed to be an escape for anyone from a universal verdict of guilt. But that isn't the end of the story. There is more to the

Law than a guilty verdict. The Law establishes patterns of atonement, and it points us toward forgiveness again and again.

One frequently described pattern of sacrifice and atonement involves people laying their hands on an animal—to signal the transfer of their guilt—before it is sacrificed.[48] Specifically, the law of Atonement required three animals—a bull and two male goats. First, the priest offered the bull as a sin offering for himself, so he would be "clean" enough to offer sacrifice for the people. He then cast lots between the two goats. One goat would be sacrificed as a way of cleansing all the elements involved in the atonement ceremony—like we rinse a dirty sponge before we use it to clean the kitchen counter.

The other goat became the "scapegoat." The priest would "lay both of his hands on the head" of the scapegoat, and "confess over it" the sins, iniquities and transgressions of all the people, just as Jesus bore our "griefs" and "the sins of many" on the Cross.[49] The sin-bearing goat was then led "away into the wilderness," just as Jesus carried away our sins.

**If we remove sacrifice for sins from the Law, we strip the Law of mercy and atonement.**

*Legalism* doesn't want us to see God Almighty sending His Son to earth to be our Scapegoat.[50] It wants us to lose sight of Jesus, who "gave Himself" as "an offering and sacrifice,"[51] "a ransom for all,"[52] "to redeem us from every lawless deed."[53] God did *not* simply give us commands. When our wise and righteous Father warned us away from the death-dealing power of sin, He also explained ways in which those sins, once committed, could be nullified.

If we remove sacrifice for sins from the Law, we completely distort what God wrote—and why. We strip the Law of mercy and atonement. We paint a grim and forbidding picture of God sitting stern and staid on His throne, more interested in His rules than in His people.[54] We shrink the Law of Moses to penalties and punishment—the elixir of false prophets and heretics who follow the teachings of the *Spirit of the Pharisee*.

The Law is far more about relieving guilt than pronouncing it. Sin does disqualify people from an eternity with God, but Christ's death cancels out sin's power to block our relationship with Him.[55] He is determined to redeem and restore any who are willing; He is eager to forgive and "cleanse us from all unrighteousness"—no matter how persistent or great.[56]

That is what God is like.

---

1  Psalm 119:68
2  Matthew 5:45
3  Psalm 25:8
4  1 Samuel 15:29; Malachi 3:6
5  Deuteronomy 6:3
6  Deuteronomy 6:18
7  Deuteronomy 6:19
8  Deuteronomy 6:2
9  John 3:16; 1 Timothy 2:6
10  Genesis 2:9
11  See Romans 1:28-31
12  Romans 7:14
13  Genesis 1:1,4; Job 26:10
14  Psalm 104:9; Jeremiah 5:22
15  Psalm 147:2-3, 19-20
16  Deuteronomy 4:7-8
17  Deuteronomy 4:40
18  Exodus 3:7; 1 Kings 8:16; Zechariah 13:9
19  2 Samuel 7:23
20  Deuteronomy 4:8; Romans 3:2
21  Exodus 19:5
22  1 Corinthians 5:5
23  Hebrews 12:8-10
24  Genesis 2:4; Psalm 89:11; Isaiah 44:24; Acts 17:24
25  Deuteronomy 4:40
26  Deuteronomy 28:1-3
27  Psalm 25:4-6
28  Proverbs 14:12
29  Isaiah 2:2
30  Isaiah 60:3
31  Deuteronomy 4:6
32  Micah 4:2
33  1 Timothy 1:8-11
34  James 1:13-15
35  Hebrews 4:15
36  Romans 5:13

37  Galatians 3:19
38  Romans 7:7
39  Romans 7:7
40  Romans 7:14
41  Romans 3:19, 23
42  Romans 5:20
43  James 2:10
44  Galatians 3:22
45  Matthew 5:20ff
46  Leviticus 15:31
47  Leviticus 26:1-13
48  Leviticus 16:5ff
49  Isaiah 53:4, 12; 1 Peter 2:24
50  Galatians 4:4-5; 1 John 4:9-10, 14
51  Ephesians 5:2
52  1 Timothy 2:6
53  Titus 2:14
54  Matthew 12:1-14
55  Colossians 2:13-14
56  1 John 1:9

# Chapter 10

# A Prophecy, a Copy and a Forgery

---

A paraphrase of one of my favorite verses reads: "The thoughts, plans, and purposes of God are very deep; senseless and spiritually insensitive people have no understanding of what He is truly up to."[1] When we judge or question God, it's usually because we do not understand what He is really doing; we interpret what we can see of His actions, and too quickly presume we understand the full picture. Looking back often gives us a better view of His dealings, but even from that perspective, it is easy to forget just how little we grasp.

We are like Job. He was a good man who feared God and perhaps understood His ways better than most other people. But when God asks Job about such things as laying "the foundation of the earth," causing "the dawn to know its place," and clothing a horse's "neck with a mane,"[2] Job realizes he understands next to nothing.

Then God asks, "Will you really annul My judgment? Will you condemn Me that you may be justified?"

In preparation for my lectures in Greece, and the subsequent writing of this book, I found the need to repent often. I didn't feel rejected by God; I simply realized (more than once) how magnificent God's work is—compared to my limited grasp of it. Much of my longing to be freed from feelings of guilt and shame was centered on myself. I wanted to be rid of that guilt, and I didn't really care how. That made me spiritually reckless in many ways throughout my Christian life.

Perhaps you can identify with me. I wanted relief from the guiltiness and self-reproach, but I wasn't particularly eager to learn anything new. Rather than asking to understand what I was missing of His marvelous plan to save an ever-sinful world, I just repeated again and again, "Please God, forgive me; I'm so sorry God. I promise I'll never do it again. Please, God, forgive me . . ."

> **I wanted relief from the guiltiness and self-reproach, but I wasn't particulaly eager to learn anything new.**

That is not a bad prayer. You probably pray something similar, and I'm sure you are equally sincere. But can you hear the note of impatience in my prayer—if not in yours? Can you see the reluctance to change my thinking (the literal meaning of *repent*), or to have my eyes opened any further? Frankly, I wanted the same quick-fix answer I've been telling you, throughout this book, isn't possible. I didn't want to bother with *complexity*—especially if I had to change my thinking—on my way to *simplicity*. Part of me judged God unfair because He wouldn't resolve my angst with the snap of His finger.

Eventually, though, it began to occur to me that I might be getting stuck not because I was such a bad sinner, but because God is such an eager Teacher. What if He wanted to open my eyes to behold "wonderful things" from His word?[3] My limited and skewed view of God's ways and His judgment made me more vulnerable than I needed to be to spiritual deception. The *Spirit of the Pharisee* kept me in an unsteady stance by peppering my thoughts with half-truths and arguments that were based on unbiblical notions (I didn't realize how unbiblical).

Without completely rethinking my thinking—and examining it in the light of God's word—I would never have been able to identify the many benefits of the Law. Once I grasped that the Law is a great deal more than an elaborate list of rights and wrongs, and the more I realized the rich purposes for the Law, the more it made sense in God's grand scheme of things.

In this chapter, I want to highlight two more aspects of the Law to explain not only why God gave the Law, but why He waited 430 years after He spoke His promise to Abraham and established faith as the basis of righteousness. Why did God institute a temporary jurisdiction for the *law of behavior* when He had already established the *law of belief?*

> **Why did God institute a temporary jurisdiction for the *law of behavior* when He had already established the *law of belief?***

## The Law As Prophecy

Have you ever tried to explain precisely what Jesus meant when He said He didn't come to "abolish the law, but to fulfill it"?[4] For years it stumped me because I had an either/or perspective on the Law and Grace. They seemed incompatible with one another. I viewed the two as opposites or competing administrations. By the way, did you catch that I misquoted the verse? I did so purposefully because most believers unknowingly leave out a significant part of what Jesus actually said, and what they leave out is the key to what He meant:

> Do not think that I came to abolish the Law or the Prophets; I did not come to abolish but to fulfill them.     —Matthew 5:17

No one imagines that Jesus' life/ministry are incompatible with Isaiah, Jeremiah, or any of the Old Testament prophets. Those books speak of Him and foreshadow His coming. Jesus didn't do away with the Prophets or the Psalms (the other two parts of Scripture before the New Testament); He lived out what they said of Him long years before He was born in Bethlehem, as written by the prophet Micah.[5] Hundreds of prophecies from the Old Testament are completed, accomplished, and fulfilled in Christ. On the final trip to Jerusalem before the crucifixion, Jesus explained to His disciples that "all things which are written through the prophets about the Son of Man will be accomplished."[6]

In my personal Bible study, as I reexamined the Law and Grace, I noted a pattern that you likely already spotted. In every instance when Jesus "fulfilled" words, those words were prophecies. In addition to the many specific prophecies in the Prophets and the Psalms, the Law also prophesied of Christ.[7] The whole Law is one big prophecy. The Law introduces atonement and sacrifice, so it perfectly foreshadows Christ as the "one sacrifice for sins for all time."[8]

When Philip told Nathanael about Jesus, he said, "We have found Him of whom Moses in the Law and also the Prophets wrote."[9] Moses gave Israel the tablets of stone and all the ordinances from God,[10] but he also prophesied about a "messenger" who would "prepare" the way of Messiah.[11] That messenger was John the Baptist, who pointed to Jesus, announcing, "Behold the Lamb of God who takes away the sin of the world."[12] Jesus fulfills the whole Law just like He fulfills other prophecies. That's why He chided the Pharisees, "If you believed Moses, you would believe Me, for he wrote about Me."[13]

**The prophetic message of the Law is that Jesus' sacrifice covers every conceivable transgression.**

Unfortunately, most followers of Jesus still think of the Law as a list of impossible-to-keep commands and impossible-to-resist sins. But viewed as an extended prophecy, the Law—with its many provisions for sacrifice and atonement—transforms the impossible list into the most profound assurance. The prophetic message of the Law is that Jesus' sacrifice covers every conceivable transgression—no matter how grievous or frequent.

For any and every violation of the Law, Jesus is the prescribed means of atonement. He is the One "whom God displayed publicly as a propitiation" for all sin.[14] He is the unblemished Lamb of God.[15] He is the scapegoat upon whom our sins are placed—and removed far from us.[16]

Contrary to what many of us have been led to believe by the *Spirit of the Pharisee*, the Law—as God intentionally wrote it—is a promise "to all the nations" of deliverance and "forgiveness of sins" in Messiah's name.[17] Instead of being impossible to keep on every point, the Law becomes a promise of forgiveness at every point of failure.

**The Law As Shadow**

In addition to being a prophecy of things to come, the Law is also a copy of things not seen. Heaven and earth are not the same realms. God is Lord of both,[18] but the kingdom of man no longer mirrors the Kingdom of God. The moment Adam and Eve were cast from the Garden, the two dimensions of reality—natural and spiritual—were torn apart. The natural sphere is at odds with the spiritual reality from which it came.[19]

Whereas before the Fall of Man, God walked and talked with our race—speaking directly to us about His plans and provisions for life—after the *sin-force* broke the world apart, we ended up worlds apart. His understanding became inscrutable;[20] His greatness and judgments unsearchable;[21] His deep wisdom and ways impenetrable to us on planet earth, severed as we were from His original plans."[22] The visible world was out of touch with the invisible, and God's ways were utterly alien and "unfathomable" to His kids.[23]

> A natural person simply cannot grasp spiritual reality.

Yet God still loved us and wanted to make Himself known to us. I know it sounds ridiculous to say it like this, but this presented Him with a sizeable problem: how was He to communicate with us since we were so estranged, so alienated from Him?

A natural person simply cannot grasp spiritual reality.[24] In order to even see the Kingdom of God—much less *enter* it—we need to be "born again" in a different dimension.[25] Flesh is flesh; spirit is spirit. Natural thoughts and perspectives aren't necessarily evil and nasty; they're just unspiritual and inadequate.

Because things in the spiritual dimension are "inexpressible" and too wonderful for earthly comprehension,[26] God needed to transpose (or copy) them from heavenly to earthly composition, so people could understand them. Through the ages, He used several means to paint pictures of heavenly realities on an earthly canvas.[27] For instance, (1) our conscience and (2) the beauty of Creation are earth-bound mediums, but both display God's "invisible attributes, His eternal power and divine nature."[28]

That isn't a difficult concept to wrap our arms around—especially when we think about how God sent His Son "in the flesh,"[29] to dwell among us,[30] so we could behold the "One who sent Him."[31] Though "He existed in the form of God," He descended into the earthly realm, clothed in the stuff of this life, and took on "the likeness of men."[32] He is the (one and only) earthly "image of the invisible God,"[33] and the precise replica of God's nature.[34] Jesus explained, "He who has seen Me has seen the Father."[35] Jesus was translated into the natural realm, where the apostles and so many others "looked at and touched [Him]."[36]

Spirit must become flesh to be grasped by flesh. It's good doctrine, and something every believer understands quickly and easily. Christ became an earthly copy of heavenly reality.

In exactly the same way, the Law was "a copy and shadow of heavenly things,"[37] but "not the very form of [those] things."[38] Everything in the Law—from the materials and measurements of the Tabernacle, to the prescriptions for our worship and behavior—corresponds to spiritual substances and dimensions. Thus, God warned Moses, "Make all things according to the pattern shown you on the mountain."[39] The earthly replica had to match the heavenly reality. The shadow cast on earth needed to have the shape of things in Heaven.

Consequently, the Law is an exact reflection of spiritual righteousness. But no matter how precise and faithful to the true, the Law of Moses is still just a copy. As righteous as the Law is, it remains no more than "a mere shadow of what is to come."[40] In today's language, the Law was made on a copy machine, and the pages God gave us were not the original. So, the

Law is (1) a prophecy of God's eternal plan for righteousness; and, (2) a copy of heavenly righteousness.

## A Partial Copy

And now I must let you in on a surprising fact about the Law. Have you ever made a copy on a copier machine when your fingers blacked out part of the copy because of how you held the original? When God made the Law-as-copy, He did that— except on purpose. Not only was the Law He gave Moses a mere copy of heavenly things,[41] it was an incomplete copy. The Law never revealed the whole picture on earth as it was in heaven.

**The Law was made on a copy machine, and the pages God gave us were not the original.**

What did God hide from view when He made the copy? The Law did not disclose His ultimate plan for salvation. The complete picture of salvation was hidden from the past ages and generations,[42] even from angels.[43] Before the ages, God predestined the full Gospel plan for redemption, but He kept it a mystery,[44] a hidden wisdom.[45] The entirety of God's plan for salvation was kept secret, and was only made known through faith at the proper time.[46]

Jesus told His disciples, "Many prophets and righteous men desired to see what you see, and did not see it, and to hear what you hear, and did not hear it."[47] Indeed, "the prophets who prophesied of the grace that would come . . . made careful searches and inquiries, seeking to know what person or time the Spirit of Christ within them was indicating."[48] Paul tells us that "mystery which has been hidden from the past ages and generations . . . has now been manifested" to us.[49]

God covered over the faith-portion of the picture because He did not want us to be confused. Commands are not promises. The commands in the Law are not "contrary to God's promises," but they never had the same life-giving power as the promises.[50] Commands cannot restore life; they cannot revitalize anyone's relationship with God, nor can they quicken people who are "dead in [their] trespasses and sin."[51] Faith in God's promises has always been the exclusive means for securing God's approval,[52] and coming alive together with Christ by grace.[53] Obedience to commands never substitutes for faith in promises.

> **Obedience to commands never substitutes for faith in promises.**

Some of our vulnerability to the *Spirit of the Pharisee* comes from supposing that God set up the Law and Grace as alternatives to one another. They are not two tools for the same job or two paths to the same destination. The writer of Hebrews explicitly tells us that "the Law made nothing perfect" because it was only a shadow of perfect things to come (i.e., the gospel message of righteousness by faith).[54] That which itself is incomplete cannot possibly complete us.

**A Temporary Pattern**

Can you see what a wobbly support the Law is for followers of Christ? Besides, in addition to being an incomplete copy, the Law is just a temporary arrangement instituted long after "the promises were spoken to Abraham and his seed."[55] Coming more than 400 years after the promise of righteousness by faith, it did not nullify the promise or invalidate the previous covenant. The temporary jurisdiction God gave to the *law of behavior* never replaced the overall jurisdiction of the *law of belief.* The Law of commands only held sway until "the fullness of time" came "when God sent forth His Son."[56] Perhaps I can best illustrate this point with an example.

My mother was quite a seamstress—and a most fashionable dresser. She sewed all of her own outfits (I learned later in life that lack of money was more motivation than love of sewing). From pictures in fashion catalogs, she selected a dress and then bought the pattern (and fabric). The patterns came in 5" x 7" envelopes and had to be unfolded piece by piece. The thin, brownish paper wasn't much to look at, but she pinned each piece of the pattern to the fabric, cut along the lines and eventually sewed all the parts together.

I was amazed such paper could be transformed into killer dresses. I don't remember what she did with the patterns once they had done their duty. But after the dress hangs in your closet, who needs the pattern? God designs and makes "garments of salvation" for every believer in Christ.[57] Just as it makes no sense to pin thin pieces of a dress pattern to an already-sewn garment, it makes no sense to affix pieces of the Law to our "robe[s] of righteousness."

The earthly blueprint we call the Law is useful—but not for those who already have the spiritual outfit from which the copy was made. Starting over once the dress has already been made is going backward. "Shrinking back" from faith was a temptation for those 1st Century believers,[58] and you, too, will sometimes be tempted to "throw away your confidence" in God's promise and grace.

By now you're getting the picture of just how incapable the Law has always been to make us righteous before God. While it is a stunningly powerful prophecy about the promise of the Messiah's work to redeem the world, the Law is not the Savior Himself. It is an incomplete and temporary copy of eternal things. When we use the Law incorrectly—trying to establish our righteousness on the basis of obedience to commands—it interferes with the relationship God wants with us, which is based on faith in His promise.

## Self-Righteousness—A Forgery

Using the Law to sustain our intimate connection with God is like using the wrong size wrench to loosen a bolt. If the wrench is just slightly too large, all it does is strip the head and make it very difficult for even the right size wrench to work afterward. The enemy knows that, and that is why if we are "ignorant" of the methods used to entrap us, evil-spirited beings can "take advantage" of us.[59]

We are much too trusting of our inner thoughts and feelings; the enemy of our soul is a master ventriloquist who uses our "sick" hearts to mislead us from paths of true righteousness.[60] When "guilty" is more than a verdict and becomes an endless mood, an inescapable prison where we spend our days, it's likely that we are listening to a lie.

> When "guilty" is more than a verdict and becomes an endless mood, it's likely that we are listening to a lie.

You are familiar with another sort of copy, an illicit one—a counterfeit or a forgery. People make that sort of copy when they do not have proper authorization. *Legalism* operates largely on falsehoods, and it passes phony bills on to unsuspecting customers like us.

One of those counterfeits is self-righteousness.

Self-righteousness, as the word implies, is something I achieve through my own effort or skill or obedience. A "righteousness of my own derived from the Law" is a stark contrast to "the righteousness which comes from God on the basis of faith."[61] Most of us presume that the distressing remorse, the lingering self-reproach that makes us feel as though God wants little to do with us, is the direct result of sins we committed. Actually, it often stems from self-righteousness, not true righteousness.

## Judging Others

In order to lure us into self-righteousness, the *Spirit of the Pharisee* taps into a fundamental sinfulness in our nature—the desire to be better (than others). It may not be a conscious attempt, but we reinforce our claim to goodness by passing judgment on people who have done what we would never do.

All of us are vulnerable to the temptation to judge (condemn) others and justify ourselves. We see this tendency even in a prison, where forgers say, "At least I don't murder people," and murderers partially excuse themselves by vilifying child molesters. Inside traders only steal from those rich enough to afford it; gang members are loyal; alcoholics aren't addicted to pornography; etc.

People condemn the tyrants of history because Hitler, Stalin, and other villains were the "worst of the worst." No rational person denies that judgment "rightly falls upon those who practice" such despicable crimes,[62] and no "good" person excuses their evil. By condemning exceptionally bad individuals, we subtly congratulate ourselves for not being like them. Deep down, we're hoping to "escape judgment" (since what we have done isn't as bad as what someone else has done).[63]

Do you recall the parable Jesus told about those who "trusted in themselves that they were righteous, and viewed others with contempt"?[64] The Pharisee in Jesus' story thanked God that he was "not like other people: swindlers, unjust, adulterers, or even like this tax collector." The acknowledged sinner, on the other hand, pled with God for mercy. Jesus ended His parable by saying that the guilty tax collector, "rather than the other," would be justified.

The Pharisees' religion divided humanity into two distinct categories: righteous and unrighteous. Those who kept the Law belonged to one group, and those who broke the Law fell into the other. The Pharisees distanced themselves from contaminated, unrighteous people because saying, "I'm not like those unrighteous people," was their way of claiming righteousness.[65] Their backward logic was simple: since people are either righteous or unrighteous, not being among the unrighteous is proof of being among the righteous. *If I am not counted among the "bad people," I must be with the "good (enough) people."*

**As long as we can spot others who are doing worse than we are, we feel safe.**

135

Judging others by contrasting our moral or religious record with theirs seems to offer us protection from judgment. We don't know exactly where the "cut-off line" may be between "good" and "bad" people, but as long as we can spot others who are doing worse than we are, we feel relatively safe. The *Spirit of the Pharisee* teaches its perverse catechism to our heart, by getting us to say, *God, I thank You that I am not like [those] other people.*[66] We highlight their favor-losing sins to gain favor for ourselves.

Obviously, such judgment is not from God. The Law places everyone in the same guilty-and-awaiting-punishment state as the despots of history, and Jesus warned against looking for the "speck" in someone else's eye.[67] It is foolish to suppose that when we "pass judgment on those who practice such things and do the same [ourselves], that [we] will escape the judgment of God."[68]

## Judging Ourselves

I realize, dear reader, that you already know that when you "judge another, you condemn yourself."[69] But, rehearsing that obvious fact helps me explain why many of those crushing feelings of guiltiness continue to overwhelm your spiritual confidence. Much of the guiltiness that stokes your fears and gnaws at your heart is a by-product of self-condemnation, the reverse side of the self-righteousness coin.

The *Spirit of the Pharisee* encourages us to judge ourselves as much as it tempts us to judge others.

The Pharisee in Jesus' parable poured contempt on sinners and deemed them unacceptable to God. After all, Law-keepers have favor with God; Law-breakers do not. The *Spirit of the Pharisee* tricks sincere believers into that same two-category mentality—about ourselves. Follow its twisted logic and catechism in your mind, and you will see what I mean.

*Legalism* craves judgment. Whereas God is patient and long-suffering and merciful in order to stay judgment as long as possible, the *Spirit of the Pharisee* wants a trial and a (guilty) verdict whenever possible.[70] Insisting on distinction between the righteous and the unrighteous, it sets itself up as a judge between two parties—one guilty and the other not guilty. Because there are two groups, the innocence of one group can be proven by the guilt of the other. Denouncing the unrighteous announces the righteous.

That's why *legalism* always presses for a guilty verdict. If one party is guilty, the other is innocent. Can you see what happens when the two parties are both us? If we let ourselves cross far beyond acceptable boundaries (*just this once*), or cave in to petty temptations to gossip, envy or fear, or when we do what we know we shouldn't do, what then.

> **We make an effort to right our wrongs by condemning our sinner-selves.**

Urged on by the *Spirit of the Pharisee*, one part of us judges the other. *I'll-never-do-it-again* attempts to escape judgment by condemning *I-did-it*. We make an effort to right our wrongs by condemning our sinner-selves. We try to deflect judgment by pointing a finger—at ourselves.

This is how *legalism* works to create lingering self-reproach. Self-condemnation is an act of self-righteousness. We're not doing it consciously, but when we "pass judgment,"[71] even against ourselves, we transform ourselves from a defendant standing trial into a judge conducting it. We are no longer "a doer of the Law but a judge of it,"[72] and God won't sanction that.[73] Plaintiffs who hope for mercy are supposed to confess, not judge.

Self-condemnation is neither a confession of wrongdoing, nor a plea for mercy. It is counterfeit religion, a false doctrine taught by the *Spirit of the Pharisee*.

---

[1] Psalm 92:5-6
[2] Job 38:4, 12; 39:19
[3] Psalm 119:18
[4] Matthew 5:17
[5] Matthew 2:5-6

6   Luke 18:31
7   Matthew 11:13; Luke 24:44
8   Hebrews 10:12
9   John 1:45
10  John 1:17
11  Deuteronomy 18:15, 18
12  John 1:29
13  John 5:46
14  Romans 3:25
15  Exodus 12:5; 1 Peter 1:17-19
16  Leviticus 16:21-22
17  Luke 24:47
18  Deuteronomy 10:14; Isaiah 44:24; Hebrews 1:10
19  Hebrews 11:3
20  Isaiah 40:28
21  Psalm 145:3
22  Romans 11:33
23  Job 9:10
24  1 Corinthians 2:14
25  John 3:3, 5
26  2 Corinthians 12:4; Ephesians 3:18-19
27  Ephesians 1:3
28  Romans 1:19-20
29  1 John 4:2
30  John 1:14
31  John 12:45
32  Philippians 2:6-8
33  2 Corinthians 4:4; Colossians 1:15
34  Hebrews 1:3
35  John 14:9
36  1 John 1:1
37  Hebrews 8:5
38  Hebrews 10:1
39  Hebrews 8:5
40  Colossians 2:17
41  Hebrews 8:5
42  Ephesians 3:9
43  1 Peter 1:12
44  Ephesians 6:19; Colossians 4:3
45  1 Corinthians 2:7
46  Romans 16:25-26
47  Matthew 13:17
48  1 Peter 1:10-11
49  Colossians 1:26
50  Galatians 3:21

51 Ephesians 2:1
52 Hebrews 11:2ff
53 Ephesians 2:5
54 Hebrews 7:19; 10:1
55 Galatians 3:16
56 Galatians 3:19; 4:4
57 Isaiah 61:10
58 Hebrews 10:38-39
59 2 Corinthians 2:11
60 Jeremiah 17:9
61 Philippians 3:9
62 Romans 2:2
63 Romans 2:3
64 Luke 18:9-14
65 Mark 7:1ff
66 Luke 18:11
67 Matthew 7:3-5
68 Romans 2:3
69 Romans 2:1
70 Psalm 145:8-9; Romans 2:4; 1 Timothy 1:16; 1 Peter 3:20; 2 Peter 3:9, 15
71 Romans 2:1
72 James 4:11
73 James 4:12

# Chapter 11

# Conviction, Condemnation and Weed-Chopping

A t that point in my Athens lecture, Angela slowed her translation and kept looking at me while speaking. Her eyes entreated, *Are you sure you want me to say that?* She was a bit puzzled—as were my Greek friends. After all the buildup and promise to answer why believers labor under terrible guilt, was I really going to blame them for being self-righteous? Wasn't that just one more thing about which to feel guilty and shamed? *Now I am supposed to feel guilty about feeling guilty?*

*No. No. No.* I wanted to plead. *You are completely missing my point.*

Instead, I simply continued, "I'm not blaming you or accusing you. I'm trying to explain that God's great love and grace will not allow you to comfortably fall into self-righteousness. A large portion of the grief and anxiety you feel is a warning sign telling you how toxic such self-condemnation is to your relationship with Him. Just as our bodies become nauseous and try to expel harmful foodstuffs, so our spirits recoil against legalistic, self-righteous thought patterns."

Self-righteousness and self-condemnation are flip sides of the same coin. If we have one, we're likely afflicted with the other. Self-condemnation is far more discomforting to us than self-righteousness, so it more readily gets our attention. A lingering sense of our unworthiness is supposed to warn us that something is very, very wrong—not with us, but with how we think about God and real righteousness.

## Conviction vs. Condemnation

*What about conviction by the Holy Spirit?* you might be asking. *Doesn't godly sorrow cause us to feel regret for the wrongs in our lives?* Yes it does, but there is a world of difference between conviction of the Holy Spirit and condemnation of the evil-spirited.

God's Spirit regularly convicts us of sin; that's one of His main jobs on earth.[1] Wrongs in our soul grieve the Spirit. As a result of bad choices we make, we "feel" some of the Spirit's grief over what we have done to others or ourselves. The mourning and unsettledness in our heart is one of the ways the Holy Spirit alerts us to sin's danger. The Spirit makes us "sorrowful to the point of repentance,"[2] and the whole point of such sorrow is to ensure that we do not, in the long run, "suffer loss in anything."[3] Godly grief inspired by God's Spirit leads to great gain. Being convicted is more about guidance than judgment.

God loves to lead His people out of their sin; the Accuser wants us left in it. That simple truth is one of the best ways to distinguish between the sorrows and pangs of conscience caused by God's love, *and* the blaming/shaming condemnation spawned by the evil-spirited. Godly sorrow motivates us to change our future behavior. Conversely, the deep mourning caused by the *Spirit of the Pharisee* immobilizes us with shame for our past behavior. God's whisper points us forward; the enemy's murmur faces us backward.

The agitated heartache we sometimes feel is one of the ways the Holy Spirit warns us away from paths of death, and "guides [us] in the paths of righteousness."[4] He "restores" our soul—meaning He turns us back from false and death-dealing ways—by convicting us. But, conviction by the Holy Spirit is not a protracted replay of our wrongs. Instead, it offers a way to end sin's power over us.

In the midst—or aftermath—of our sin, spiritual conviction produces "a repentance without regret, leading to [more] salvation."[5] Repentance "without regret" means that we don't spend lots and lots of time regretting what we did. Should we feel sorry about what we did? Yes, of course. When feeling badly about our sin turns into all-is-lost sorrow and self-reproach, however, it usually means the *Spirit of the Pharisee* has hijacked our repentance.

> **God's arrangement for dealing with our wrongdoing is simple: the Spirit convicts; we repent and confess; God forgives.**

God's chief desire is to have relationship with us, and He sacrificed everything He held dear in order to secure us to Himself. God's arrangement for dealing with our wrongdoing is simple: the Spirit convicts; we repent and confess; God forgives.

End of story.

When He convicts you, the Holy Spirit isn't putting you on probation. Rather, He puts your sin on notice, and begins sort of a spiritual countdown, numbering your sin's days and announcing its sure demise. Godly conviction is like a wanted poster in an old western town: The picture on the poster is not your face, but that of your sin.

Conviction is like a notice from your credit card company warning you of fraudulent use of your account. The Spirit asks you, "Do you want/ authorize these transactions?" Answering "No" is the essence of repentance. Conviction heightens your sensitivity to "identity theft" and urges you toward more careful behavior.

And that brings me back to the goodness of God whose "kindness and tolerance and patience" lead us to repentance—not condemnation.[6] Jesus' offer of righteousness is based on forgiveness. When we acknowledge that we have (once again) done wrong—and ask for His forgiveness—we are making use of the primary element of God's *righteous-by-faith* covenant. We are partaking of Jesus' righteousness, not tapping into our own supply. We are living under the provisions of the *law of belief.*

## Salvation "Security"

Is it fitting to thank Jesus over and over for His forgiveness? Yes. Is it wise to rehearse our vulnerabilities that led us into the sin—so that we can posture ourselves in repentance to be less vulnerable in the future? Yes, of course. But a longing for more obedience in our future is not the same thing as condemning ourselves for the past.

Can people become so hardened and calloused in heart—overwhelmed by the deceitfulness of sin—that they make a conscious choice to reject Christ's salvation gift? Can people who once accepted Messiah's sacrificial death for their sins, turn around and knowingly refuse the rescue they once embraced?

Yes, I believe that some who were once believers can come to such a place of deception in their lives that they elect to believe no longer. But it is their conscious choice, not God's.

I'm not talking about people who carry on too long in sin, but people who consciously decide they do not want or need Christ's forgiveness. Since we stand only by our faith, those who turn from belief to unbelief "throw away [their] confidence,"[7] and will be broken off from eternity with Him.[8] That's why we have "need of endurance."[9] If we endure in faith, we will receive what God promised, and we will "also reign with Him."[10] The consequence for unbelief—regardless of when a person chooses not to believe—is the same: eternal separation from God.

> A longing for more obedience in our future is not the same thing as condemning ourselves for the past.

You may be aware that within the Body of Christ there are two differing views on the "safety" of believers' salvation, and I do not wish to enter that debate in strident tones. Essentially there are those who believe (1) individuals have been predestined to salvation, and no matter what they do or believe after they come to Christ, if they are saved, they are saved forever. In their view, the horrifically backslidden (i.e. those who supposedly came to Christ, then subsequently seem to reject Him by protracted sinfulness) were never truly children of God in the first place.

Others in the Church believe (2) individuals remain free agents with a will to choose or reject salvation up until the moment they die because, as image bearers of God, they have been assigned a will; the ability to choose for or against Christ is not stripped away by salvation. In their view willful/continual disobedience (i.e. long-term wandering in sin) can harden someone to such an extent that a person could willfully choose to reject Christ and "shrink back to destruction."[11] This has mistakenly been called "losing" their salvation.

In laymen's lingo, these perspectives are cryptically known as "Eternal Security" and "Eternal Insecurity."[12] That's not really fair to either group.

> **I never need worry that my sin is too gross for forgiveness, or that my wrongs will cut off contact with God.**

Regardless of a Christian's view of their eternal "security," I've noticed that both groups worry, at times, that their relationship with Him might be interrupted or suspended: (1) *If extreme backsliders "weren't really ever saved," then my recent mess-up might be proof that I'm not really saved;* or, (2) *If I am free to choose or reject Christ throughout my life, then my continued wrestling with sin/bondage might be proof that I have denied Him (with my deeds).*

## Salvation by Faith

Relationship with God does not depend on our ability to behave perfectly—or even fairly well (compared to others). Before we were baptized into Christ's death, we could not possibly have restored lost relationship with God through obedience to His commands. Consequently, the restored relationship cannot be lost due to disobedience to His commands. I never need worry that my sin is too gross for forgiveness, or that my wrongs will cut off contact with God.

Access to God is through belief, not behavior. If, therefore, people no longer believe, my personal perspective is that they no longer have eternal life with Him. They are like trapped miners hundreds of feet behind a collapsed tunnel. When a rescuer finds the lost miners and begins leading them to safety, we can say the miners have been saved. However, if at some point along the rescue route, some miners dodge away from the rescuer and refuse to follow him to safety, those miners are lost again—not because of the tunnel collapse, but because of their decision to reject the rescue.

God is relentless in His pursuit of us and in His provision to cover our sin with the shed blood of His Son. No matter how much we sin, His blood is more than enough covering; but if we refuse the covering, we're no longer covered. We cannot exhaust the supply of forgiveness, but we can refuse it.

## Chopping Weeds

In no way do I want to communicate that the Law is opposed to God's purposes, or that the Law is bad. As we saw, the Law of Moses, what I call the *law of behavior*, did many things well: it acted as an offsetting power to the *sin-force* that corrupted the world, and it gave specific guidance to God's children for healthful living in a contaminated world. But I do want you to understand that the Law is inadequate for the full purposes of God in our lives.

The Law has limited usefulness. Like a physician's text of diseases and treatments, the Law details sin-symptoms and prescribes suitable remedies for relief from those symptoms. But like cold "remedies"

**Like a hoe chopping at weeds, the Law doesn't cut deep enough to get at the roots of sin.**

sold at a pharmacy, it has no real power to kill the virus causing the sore throat. The Law addresses symptoms, not causes. It can't get at our real problem.

145

Like a hoe chopping at weeds, the Law doesn't cut deep enough to get at the roots of sin.

Sin is not a surface issue. Apparently, the Pharisees thought it was. That's what misled them into imagining that if they behaved well and didn't (physically) do any of the things they weren't supposed to do, they would be considered righteous. As long as they manifested no *external* symptoms, they supposed they were not sick. Unless they were "caught in adultery, in the very act,"[13] they did not see themselves as adulterers under the Law. Externally they obeyed, but inwardly they were like everyone else.

Though they "appear[ed] righteous to men," they were full of "hypocrisy and lawlessness."[14] Jesus called the Pharisees "blind guides of the blind,"[15] and told people, "Unless your righteousness surpasses that of the scribes and Pharisees, you shall not enter the kingdom of heaven."[16] Their brand of righteousness was only skin-deep. They misinterpreted the Law of Moses as a checklist for good and bad behavior that could be used as proof of their righteousness.

## Inside and Out

Jesus did not come to abolish the Law.[17] Christ didn't limit the Law's authority or lessen the degree of guilt in people's lives. He did not make the Law less stringent, easier to obey, or irrelevant. Rather, He pinpointed new dimensions of guilt and law-breaking in everyone's heart—and held to a far more difficult measure of righteousness than anything the Pharisees understood.

> **Our hearts are infected with the *sin-force*, and no amount of external cleansing will rid us of internal dirtiness.**

According to Jesus, our heart is more to the point than our hands.[18] Our hearts are infected with the *sin-force*, and no amount of external cleansing will rid us of internal dirtiness. Regardless of how well we control our actions, that self-control does not (always) extend completely or permanently to our heart—from which come "evil thoughts, murders, adulteries, fornications, thefts, false witnesses, slanders," and other corruptions.[19]

Interesting, isn't it, that illicit *words about* someone are in the same list as illicit acts with someone?

Jesus said, "Everyone who looks at a woman with lust for her has already committed adultery with her in his heart."[20] To the Pharisees, such a statement was highly offensive because their standing with God and man was based only on behavior:[21] *"Yes, yes, you may be thinking those thoughts and committing those sins in your mind, but you are only unrighteous if you actually do them."* That is the essential lie of the religion called *legalism*: "You are only guilty of sin if you (physically) commit the sin." The Pharisees succumbed to that lie, and that's why they "trusted in themselves that they were righteous, and viewed others with contempt."[22]

Whereas the Holy Spirit convicts us of inner sins like bitterness and wrath and anger,[23] the *Spirit of the Pharisee* congratulates us for not *acting* on them. Do you see how tempting *legalism* can be? With one false stroke, it eliminates a wide swath of sin in our life because a host of wrong-spirited attitudes, imaginings, and fantasies don't get tallied as sins. Though seemingly harsh and unforgiving, *legalism* actually tempts us with a far more lax standard: if we don't act out our inner trespasses, they don't get counted against us.


## A Dangerously False Measure


Granted, done-deeds cause much more damage to other people than thought-deeds. Imagining what it would be like to murder, bed, or slander someone is far less consequential than actually doing it. A sinful thought rarely reconfigures our physical world. Fewer lives are affected by our mental sin, and it can easily be forgotten and swept from consequence in our future. It didn't ruin anyone's life; it isn't necessary to ask forgiveness or make restitution for an imagined robbery.

But as violations against God, thoughts and actions are equally offensive. Before the court of Heaven, guilt for *mental sin* and *physical sin* match each other.[24] God sees in secret[25] and all things are open and laid bare to the eyes of [God].[26] When a wicked suggestion comes to our mind, we tell ourselves, "*No. Don't do that. Don't give in to temptation.*" That is the correct response. If we avoid living out the wicked suggestion, we feel victorious—and like a good Christian.

But have we actually been victorious? Even if we manage to discipline ourselves completely, so that we never commit a sin with our physical body, can we "put confidence in the flesh"?[27] According to Jesus, often what we call a temptation is actually a mental sin. Even if we (only) undress someone with our eyes, we are guilty of sin.[28] Coveting what someone else has is as unrighteous as stealing it from them.

We might not give into temptation to take revenge physically, but we fantasize about it. We might not slander co-workers out loud, but slanderous *thoughts* about them occupy our mind. We might not follow the hinted interest of a stranger with whom we chatted after work, but (later that evening) we fantasize where and how things might have gone if we took the hint. Good for us that we didn't go there, but keeping the outside clean doesn't make the inside spotless.

> **Equating internal sins to external sins is not giving license for people to live out their fantasies; it is, instead, giving evidence for people to face up to their sinful condition.**

My point is NOT to tell you that since *sin-thoughts* are as bad as *sin-deeds*, you might just as well carry out the wicked imaginings of your heart. I am NOT telling you it doesn't matter if you do right or wrong. The New Testament tells us to "behave properly," and "lay aside the deeds of darkness."[29] Right and wrong still exist.

Equating internal sins to external sins is not giving license for people to live out their fantasies; it is, instead, giving evidence for people to face up to their sinful condition. Jesus was speaking to people who believed they had avoided infection by the *sin-force*. He was telling people that whether or not symptoms had yet appeared, they were infected with a deadly disease, nonetheless. Jesus wasn't offering license for sin (abolishing the Law); He wasn't saying right and wrong no longer matter.

## Getting at the Roots

Grace is NOT God declaring, "Anything goes."

The real issue that confronts every person is how to become righteous inside and out, righteous through and through. Jesus reminded the Pharisees that "He who made the outside [made] the inside also."[30] Keeping the Law could not cure the Pharisees' desperately sick hearts,[31] and neither can it clean ours. Obedience to rules of behavior doesn't have the cleansing power to get at our insides where sins root and grow again and again.

To the extent that we gauge how well we are doing in our walk of faith primarily by our behavior, we drift dangerously close to the teaching of the Pharisees, who "clean the outside of the cup and of the platter; but inside . . . are full of robbery and wickedness."[32] No one (else) may know of our trespass unless we are "caught in the very act,"[33] but even those found blameless according to the "righteousness which is in the Law,"[34] know they are not sinless.

The apostle Paul emphasizes this point when he explains that the Gentiles—those without the Law—did not "pursue righteousness" by being obedient to commands. And yet, they attained "the righteousness which is by faith."[35] Conversely, Israel tried to pursue righteousness by obedience to the Law, but never attained it. "Why? Because they did not pursue it by faith, but . . . by works."[36] The Jews, who had the Law, did not understand God's plan to restore righteousness among His people; instead, they sought "to establish their own" and did not rely on His provision for righteousness.[37]

Paul says his countrymen were "broken off" from the "cultivated olive tree" because of their "unbelief,"[38] but "if they do not continue in their unbelief," God will "graft them in again."[39] Faith in Christ, not obedience to the Law, establishes our righteousness in the sight of God. Faith enables all people to become righteous—even though they are soiled by "original sin."

## A Cure

Let's quickly review the spiritual timeline of history. When Adam was disobedient to God, the *sin-force* virus "entered into the world" and spread death to every person.[40] By that invasion, all were "made sinners."[41] No matter how carefully people tried to avoid contracting the virus, it was already at work in them, beginning the end of their days (and life as God meant it to be).

Nearly 2500 years elapsed from the moment the *sin-force* infected our race until God gave the Law. If He intended simply to treat the *sin-virus*, it seems most uncaring to withhold the remedy for so many centuries. On the other hand, if the opposite is true, and God didn't want anyone to confuse the *law of behavior* with a cure for the *sin-force*, then the time gap makes much more sense.

**Adam's disobedience infected us; Christ's obedience cures us. Adam made us unrighteous; Christ makes us righteous.**

God arranged a "better way" for us than onward obedience.[42] Jesus is that "new and living way" to righteousness. He replaces the Law as the means by which we are made righteous before God, and that is why the Bible says He "is the end of the law for righteousness to everyone who believes."[43]

The Law never got to the roots of our sin; neither could it address "original sin" that contaminates each of us.

Christ was "obedient to the point of death, even death on a cross,"[44] and thanks to "the obedience of the One," there is a cure for the *sin-virus*.[45] As Paul puts it, "through one transgression there resulted condemnation to all men, even so through one act of righteousness there resulted justification . . . to all men."[46]

Adam's disobedience infected us; Christ's obedience cures us. Adam made us unrighteous; Christ makes us righteous.[47]

We didn't and couldn't earn it by our efforts or hygiene protocols. We didn't get the antidote because we were good enough—or tried hard enough.[48] The cure is not a home remedy. More like a gift certificate than a packaged present, it grants the bearer "eternal life in Christ Jesus."[49] It grants eternal immunity from prosecution and judgment.[50] In the grand equation of eternity, our race wronged all that God made and intended for us. God righted that wrong, not through our individual efforts and works, but at one time for all time, He, Himself, brought salvation to all people: "He saw that there was no man . . . to intercede," so "His own arm brought salvation."[51]

## Justice?

You and I were not in the Garden. We weren't the ones whose disobedience rendered us irreversibly unrighteous. Adam's seed and blood infected us at birth—even before we violated God's commands ourselves. So, even keeping the Law of Moses perfectly will not rid us of sin. Is that justice?

No.

You and I were not at Calvary. It wasn't our obedience and death that rendered us irreversibly righteous. Christ's seed and blood cured us at rebirth. So, keeping the Law of Moses imperfectly will not infect us again with the *sin-virus*. Is that justice?

No.

Oh, praise be to God.

---

1 John 16:8
2 2 Corinthians 7:9
3 2 Corinthians 7:9
4 Psalm 23:3
5 2 Corinthians 7:10
6 Romans 2:4
7 Hebrews 10:35
8 Romans 11:20

9   Hebrews 10:36 (see also 2 Corinthians 6:4; James 1:3-4)
10  2 Timothy 2:12
11  Hebrews 10:39
12  Special thanks to Mark Chester, Chris Manginelli and Tim May for much of this language.
13  John 8:4
14  Matthew 23:28
15  Matthew 15:14
16  Matthew 5:20
17  Matthew 5:17-18
18  Matthew 12:24
19  Matthew 15:19
20  Matthew 5:28
21  Matthew 15:1-20
22  Luke 18:9
23  Ephesians 4:31
24  Matthew 5:21ff
25  Matthew 6:4, 6
26  Hebrews 4:13
27  Philippians 3:3-4
28  Matthew 5:27-28
29  Romans 13:12-13
30  Luke 11:40
31  Jeremiah 17:9
32  Luke 11:39
33  John 8:4
34  Philippians 3:6
35  Romans 9:30
36  Romans 9:31-32
37  Romans 10:3
38  Romans 11:20
39  Romans 11:23
40  Romans 5:12
41  Romans 5:19
42  Hebrews 10:20 (see Hebrews 7:19-22 and 8:6)
43  Romans 10:4
44  Philippians 2:8
45  Romans 5:19
46  Romans 5:18
47  Romans 5:19
48  Romans 4:2-5; Ephesians 2:8-9
49  Romans 6:23
50  John 3:18, 36
51  Isaiah 59:16

# Chapter 12

# The Tutor, the Test and the Twin

---

Thus far, I have left out one of the best-known explanations of the Law as "our tutor to lead us to Christ."[1] That familiar concept about the Law would have fit perfectly in the previous chapters when I spoke about the benefits and advantages the Law gives us. Perhaps you wondered why I skipped that familiar metaphor in the New Testament for the Old Covenant.

If you have ever played Scrabble, you know that when you can't find a great word to play, shifting the letter tiles around will often reveal new possibilities. By purposefully using other language to come at how the Law of Moses fits and works together with God's grace, I'm trying to put your letter tiles in a different order, so you see things in a new light. You've been staring at the board for a long time, and you truly want another way to think about things, right? Reaching different conclusions usually requires taking different routes.

How to reconcile "be good" with "be forgiven" isn't a simple subject. It is further complicated by self-reproach and those terrible, lingering feelings of guiltiness. Much of that guiltiness is spawned by the evil-spirited being that I have named the *Spirit of the Pharisee*. *Legalism*, that demon's doctrine, teaches that if we want to be (more) acceptable to God, we must sufficiently reform our behavior and maintain an adequate level of morality. If we fall short of those standards of conduct, we get put on probation under God's anger and impatience. If we do not get our acts together, it says we will ultimately "fall away."

Simplistic phrases and incomplete Scripture quotes will not help us sort things through. As I have been hinting all along in this book, sometimes the long way around is the best way to arrive at a simple understanding. So, I have intentionally avoided all the quick shortcuts, and have spent more time looking at the background to your real question (i.e. the reason you bought this book) than you may have wanted.

Images and phrases can become so familiar that they lose much of their message. That's why I held off reintroducing the Law as tutor— because we know it so well. Or, at least we think we do. You'll probably be surprised to learn that the remaining portion of the half-sentence you so familiarly quote reads, "that we may be justified by faith." Here's what Paul said:

> But before faith came, we were kept in custody under the Law, being shut up to the faith which was later to be revealed. Therefore the Law has become our tutor to lead us to Christ, so that we may be justified by faith. But now that faith has come, we are no longer under a tutor.
> —Galatians 3:23-25

> **God promises; we believe. That is the ever-present equation in all of God's dealings with people.**

As I have been telling you, faith is the key to everything God has in mind for us. He promises; we believe. That is the ever-present equation in all of God's dealings with people. Without a promise from God and faith in our hearts, we cannot possibly please Him with our behavior. However well-intentioned, our efforts in the flesh will always and only produce offspring of flesh.

The commands in the Law were never meant to be God's final words to us. As we learned in the previous chapter, the Law of Moses was a prophetic promise: God would send a Savior as a once-for-all sacrifice to take away our sins like the scapegoat into the wilderness. God sent His Son "to be the Savior of the world,"[2] and "when the kindness of God our Savior and His love for humankind appeared, He saved us, not on the basis of deeds which we have done in righteousness, but according to His mercy, by the washing of regeneration and renewing by the Holy Spirit."[3] That is what God is like.

**We don't need anyone or anything to tell us Jesus is coming when He is here in our hearts.**

All along, His plan has been to justify us "by His grace," and make us "heirs according to the hope of eternal life."[4] God's purpose "from all eternity" was "revealed by the appearing of our Savior Christ Jesus, who abolished death and brought life and immortality to light through the gospel."[5]

From Christ onward, we no longer are under the custody of the Law of Moses. The *law of behavior* was on the lookout for Christ's coming, so it could signal to us like a forward observer, "He's here. He's here, at last." We don't need anyone or anything to tell us Jesus is coming when He is here in our hearts.

## A Tutor

I began my final evening that summer in Athens by applauding the audience for making it through all the history lessons and lecture material I threw at them for three evenings. Congratulations are in order for you, too, dear reader. I'll bet there were portions of this book that almost made you feel like you were back in school. Remember those days: homework, papers, and tests?

Do you recall, as I do, certain students finishing algebra or chemistry exams early and placing them on the instructor's desk long before the class period ended? Those bright classmates answered everything on their tests; no need to wait around for those of us who couldn't—no matter how much time we had. Seemed to me like those who walked out of exams early always scored highest on the tests. I tried their test-taking technique once and discovered that the secret for a good grade is not the timing of when you turn in a test. Alas, the key is to actually know the subject material.

That's why securing the help of a good tutor can be the difference between passing and failing an examination. Knowing that His children do not naturally understand matters of spiritual life and eternity—just like some of us aren't good at science and math—God employed the services of a Tutor for our benefit. He assigned the Law of Moses to coach us for the *Final Exam of Life*—at least, the first half of it.

You did know, didn't you, that life has a *Final Exam*? Some individuals don't believe a loving God would ever evaluate people, so unfortunately, they don't prepare for the *Big Test* until it's too late. The *Final Assessment* is a BIG deal. Our answers determine our eternity. Thankfully, the *Test* is short, and designed to be finished early—before the end of our life. As soon as we know the correct answers, we can complete the *Last Exam*, turn it in, and await eternity in confidence. What relief. No more examinations. Finish this one and we are set forever.

Even for people who struggle with spiritual subjects, it's relatively easy—with just two, non-essay questions. The answer sheet has no space for long explanations. A straightforward "Yes" or "No" answers Questions #1 and #2. It's also an "open-book" *Final*, and we're welcome to study with friends. Looking over a neighbor's shoulder to view their answers is completely acceptable—and even encouraged. What could be easier?

## The First Question

I don't know if this makes the *Big Test* easier or more difficult, but researchers have observed that people who answer the first question wrong, always get the second one wrong, as well. In virtually every case, the answer people give to Question #1 is the answer they supply to Question #2.

That makes Question #1 fairly critical, doesn't it? And it explains why the hired Tutor concentrates exclusively on helping us come to the right answer for Question #1. The Tutor's job is to rehearse the correct response to that crucial question, over and over.

Question #1 is short and simple: *Are you guilty?*

To help people answer correctly, the *law of behavior* provides a legal cheat-sheet (in small print). It lists several follow-up questions like: Have you ever wronged or used another person for personal gain or satisfaction? Have you dishonored God or your parents? Have you coveted or stolen what belonged to another? In thought or action, have you murdered or assassinated anyone's character? Have you desired any except your spouse? Have you gossiped, lied, or sworn in rage? Have you judged others, lived in self-pity or bitterness? Have you underreported on your taxes, fantasized inappropriately or turned a blind eye toward those in need? You could truthfully say, the *Test* is rigged—to get correct.

The *law of behavior*, our provided-by-God Tutor, convinces us that "Yes" is the correct answer to Question #1 by faithfully pointing out when, where, and how we violate God's way. The Law rehearses our guilt like multiplication tables, so we memorize the verdict. The *Tutor of Guiltiness* uses a limited vocabulary, hardly more than a single word—"*Guilty*." That is all it needs to help you get the question right. It wants you to pass the *Big Exam*.

Presented with the clear evidence, it's surprising how long and vehemently people (like us) react with, "No, I'm not. I'm not guilty. I'm not guilty." That "Not Guilty" protest appears to be deeply imbedded in our core being and seems

**People imagine that the worst possible fate is to be found guilty. God sees it more like the diagnosis of a treatable disease.**

almost instinctual—as though we were made that way. People imagine that the worst possible fate is to be found guilty. God sees it more like the diagnosis of a treatable disease. If detected early enough, guilt can be cured.

## False Personas

By the way, a favorite ploy of the evil-spirited is to imbed counterfeit identity traits so far inside people's *sin-nature* that they believe those forged qualities are part of them. To deny those sin impulses feels like a denial of their true person. As evidence of their authenticity, those deeply deceptive roots grow and bear fruit. The more people eat that false fruit, the more those personality attributes grow and assume a "natural" place in their lives. Wrongly, those people presume that what seems so natural, must be innate—just the way they were born. The deceitful branches eventually claim a place right alongside the truly God-made limbs.

> **Pride, fear, and lawlessness create a chorus in our soul, shouting, "I am not guilty."**

The truth is that God does not pre-program people to violate His ways. We make sinners of ourselves when we "exchange the truth of God for a lie"[6] and believe what the enemy of our soul says about who and what we are. We are each made in God's image and designed to function appropriately in His created order.

Our *sin-nature*, however, is quite a fighter, and it protests its innocence to the bitter end. Pride, fear, and lawlessness create a chorus in our soul, shouting, "I am NOT guilty." One of the surest ways it presents the case of its innocence is to claim, "I'm just made this way; this is who I am."

Questions of guiltiness are deflected with defenses of identity.

Perhaps that is why the *Tutor* never really quits tutoring. The Law repeats itself like flashcards used in a rote memory lesson: "*Guilty. Guilty. Guilty.*" Even after we've learned how to answer Question #1, the Law continuously reinforces the previous tutorials: "You are guilty here, guilty there, guilty everywhere." It sometimes throws us off to keep hearing the old lesson—after we've turned in our *Exam*—but we need the reminder. Besides, we shouldn't expect the *law of behavior* to change its tune. It doesn't have much else to say to us.[7]

## The Second Question

The *Tutor* wasn't necessarily hired to teach the correct response to Question #2, and the answer seems so obvious, it's hard to imagine that anyone needs coaching to get it right. The correct answer to Question #1 (i.e. "Yes") leads perfectly to the right response to the second question on the *Big Final*.

Question #2 simply asks, *"Do you want to be forgiven?"*

The first question (*"Are you guilty?"*) is a total setup for the second (*"Do you want to be forgiven?"*) because God's plan has always been to extend grace to people who acknowledge their guilt.[8] The only ones who miss out on grace are those too proud to admit that they don't always live life right.[9] Sinners who realize their wrongdoing can hope for mercy and forgiveness in the New Covenant. Jesus the Physician comes to the sick, and He offers forgiveness to sinners, not to the righteous.[10] Jesus restores sight to those who admit they are blind, but those claiming to see (i.e. claiming not to sin), remain in their sin.[11]

> If conviction and confession of guilt lead to forgivenesss, who but a fool would deny guilt?

It's fair to say that repenting of guilt is "the beginning of the Gospel."[12] *Legalism* tries to make our guilt the end of the story—a concluding commentary on our life or ministry. If guilt surely leads to condemnation and punishment, who but a fool would willingly admit guilt? But on the other hand, if conviction and confession of guilt lead to forgiveness, who but a fool would deny guilt? That's why there are two questions on the *Final* Final.

Forgiveness doesn't apply to innocent people. Consequently, guilty people sometimes find little relief from guilty feelings because they insist too vehemently on their innocence. Until guilt is a registered fact in our soul, we won't pursue or find forgiveness.

The Law of Moses has not passed away.[13] It's still doing its job very effectively, tutoring us about our guilt. But remember, *"Guilty, Guilty,*

*Guilty"* is not the ending message of the Gospel. The Tutor (i.e. the Law) knows a great deal about guilt—and it has *hints* of redemption—but it doesn't know very much about forgiveness and grace. What the Tutor tells us is true—as far as it goes, but the Tutor's knowledge is incomplete. Even though the Gospel message was preached as early as Abraham,[14] The Law (and the Prophets) had limited understanding about the eventual plan of God to justify the guilty by faith. Only later did God entirely reveal His Son as the once-for-all-time-and-all-sin guilt offering,[15] who would "put away sin by the sacrifice of Himself."[16]

John the Baptist announced the Messiah by "preaching a baptism of repentance for the forgiveness of sins."[17] God raised Jesus "to His right hand as a Prince and a Savior, to grant repentance . . . and forgiveness of sins" to us.[18] "Guilty" is no longer the last word—unless we forget Question #2: "*Will you accept Jesus' atonement (payment) to remove your guilt?*"


## A Guardian

Unfortunately, many believers—who answered Question #2 correctly when they came to Christ—forget to answer it in their daily life. Our forgetfulness is understandable because we're still getting accustomed to our new status as full-fledged members of God's family. We're still in the process of realizing how rich we are. Until God spoke that new "promise of the Spirit" to all people,[19] the Law acted like a guardian watching over the affairs of our life. It trained us and told us what we could and could not do. We were like under-age heirs under the Law's authority.[20] "In the fullness of time," however, God sent Jesus to "redeem those who were under the law," and release us from its authority to manage our affairs.[21]

Like a woman whose husband has died, we have died to the Law and are no longer bound to it,[22] but our new state takes some getting used to. The correct answer to question #2 remains "Yes"—every day throughout our days.

## The Evil Twin

Speaking of questions, do you ever feel like you have an evil twin—someone who looks like you but actually is *Another-you* inside of *You-you*, hijacking *Real-you*?

I do. I feel like I have *Another-me* inside of me.

I'm embarrassed by the imaginings that *Another-me* (not *Real-me*) plays in my mind. Like a dazed soldier in the aftermath of a horrific battle, *Me-me* wanders about in spiritual shock, staggered by the enormous wrongdoing committed by *Twin-me*. *Real-me* has little memory of doing the wrong—or how I got to such a place in my life. I want to ask my *Twin-me*, *"Who are you; what were you thinking? What have you done; where have you taken us?"*

*That-me* appalls *This-me*. *Twin-me* shocks *Me-me*.

**Claiming to be followers of Christ, we lift our hearts in praise, and simultaneously scoop them in the gutter. We slip so quickly from victors to voyeurs.**

As earnest believers in Christ, aren't we ashamed by our weakness to resist temptation, our eagerness to jab someone with unkindness, or our gladness to see adversaries stumble? We know better and we want better, and much of the time, we even opt for the better—but not always. How can we be such hypocrites, thinking and doing what we know is wrong—but doing it anyway? We feel like spiritual imposters. Claiming to be followers of Christ, we lift our hearts in praise, and simultaneously scoop them in the gutter. We slip so quickly from victors to voyeurs.

I'll ask again, as I did in Greece, "Do you ever feel like you have an evil twin?"

No need to reply. As I rehearsed the sorts of failures common to us all, and paused to allow my friends in Greece to think back on the imaginings they had enshrined in their hearts, they sat mutely, too. Flashbacks of failure and other points of regret ignited shame in their minds. I stood mutely on the stage and left them alone with recollected secrets, replayed video clips, and memories of choices. Condemnation filled the auditorium in Greece.

I heard the gavel pounding in their fearful hearts: *Guilty. Guilty. Guilty.*

The horrid litany of guilt begins a familiar, shame-filled sequence of thoughts in our minds, doesn't it? We are tortured and damned by the truth that rings out from our innermost being, as it did from David's: "I know my transgressions; my sin is ever before me."[23]

*Guilty. Guilty. Guilty. Oh no.*

Beneath all the theology and rhetoric, this is where we live out our days, laboring under legal indictment, tempted to cower under the shrill accusations against us. Whether it is a previously undetected pattern of wickedness, a point of present willfulness, or the spillover of a long-simmering fire in our flesh, our sin disappoints us. It damns us—perhaps not to hell, but to an uneasy avoidance of our Savior. We berate ourselves: *I should have been stronger, smarter, and quicker to escape.*

Perhaps that is the main reason you purchased this book. You hoped for a way to silence the accusations. Instead, I am bringing you face-to-face with the very things you wanted gone from your soul. If we were sitting together now over coffee, I'm sure you would be reproaching me with your eyes—as though I had failed you and "outed" you as a sinner. I've exposed your dark side and the secret saboteur in your soul. You hoped for discreet counsel to make you a better Christian less prone to sin, and I've announced the contents of your brown paper sack. But there is a reason—please read on.

## Identity Theft

The reason you and I feel like we have an evil twin is because, biblically speaking, we do.

What else accounts for why you do the very things *Real-you* doesn't wish to do? What other explanation can you offer for why you fail to practice what you want to do?[24] In the deepest, most central part of your heart, you have presented yourself to God completely, and invited Him to be Lord over every part of your body and mind.[25] Yet, at the same time, you give yourself to do "the very evil" you hate.[26] You love God, and don't know why you do what you do.

As incredible as it sounds, an evil twin inhabits the same space as you.[27] Since I gave a name to the "*Spirit of the Pharisee*," I'll name this other persona in your life *E. Twin*. What you hate, it loves. What you know is wrong to do, it wants to do—and leaves you feeling like you have no choice in the matter. At the very moment when you are doing one thing, *E. Twin* can be doing exactly the opposite. That's why you sometimes feel like you're going crazy. *Twin-you* impersonates *You-you* daily, making off with your true identity and using your "credit card" (i.e. your good name) to make lurid and despicable purchases.

> *Other-self* **does what we detest–and makes us feel responsible for doing it.**

No wonder we get confused about our behavior.[28] *E. Twin*—your *Other-self*—opposes you and God's plan for your life. Even though you swear to yourself you won't let it happen again, *E. Twin* just laughs at you. *Other-self* does what we detest—and makes us feel responsible for doing it. It loves to frame us for law-breaking acts, and enjoys watching us take the blame.

Street-smart, utterly lawless and very, very evil, *E. Twin* completely disregards every intent of God's Law. "Nothing good dwells in" *Twin-me*.[29] It is determined, well-conditioned, and very strong (in the flesh), so it makes a mockery of our good intentions as it bullies and drags us along to places we don't want to be. *Fleshy-me* holds *Spirit-me* hostage to do its will.

The *Spirit of the Pharisee* knows how to quote scripture and sound so biblical. If we do not know the full truth of the Scriptures and God's plan of salvation by faith, that evil-spirited liar can trick us, just as the serpent fooled Eve. Perhaps you have heard what I heard for so many years coming from its accusing lips: "*Yes, you have been forgiven and saved by grace, but Jesus told you to go and sin no more. If you 'go on sinning willfully after receiving the knowledge of the truth, there no longer remains a sacrifice for sins.'*[30] *After all, 'No one who is born of God practices sin . . .'"*[31]

With a few well-placed verses that we only half-remember, *legalism* brings us to an inevitable conclusion: *If "no one born of God sins," and I have sinned, does that mean . . .? Have I lost—or never truly had—relationship with God? Since I do the things God hates, does He now hate me? I still sin; am I still saved?*

*Oh no. Guilty. Guilty. Guilty.*


## Identity Protection

Grace reaches the same verdict as the Law—but for a different defendant. God indicts *Other-me* instead of *Me-me* as the guilty party. That was the life-changing realization the apostle Paul came to when he considered the undeniable sin in his own life. Follow his reasoning, and claim it as your own:

1. I agree with the Law of Moses, that an unrighteous, wicked thing has been thought or done;
2. The fingerprints and DNA traces found at the scene of the sin point to me;
3. But I do not want to do such a thing; it is "the very thing I hate;"[32]
4. Since it is "the very thing I do not wish" in my life, then someone other than me must be "the one doing it."[33]
5. The DNA is nearly identical to mine, so it must belong to *E. Twin*.
6. *E. Twin* is guilty; there is, therefore, no condemnation for me.[34]

*Guilty. Guilty. Guilty.* Oh yes. Absolutely guilty—*Twin-me*, not *Me-me*.

"No one born of God sins" is not a threat, or a measure against which you and I are to be judged by the *Spirit of the Pharisee* and its prophets. Quite the contrary: it is the single greatest promise in the New Covenant.

When we received Christ as Savior, we were "born again." That's how and why we are able to see and enter the Kingdom of God.[35] Being "found in Him, not having a righteousness of [our] own derived from the Law, but that which is through faith in Christ,"[36] we became new creations.[37] Simply put, we were born of God.[38]

Before you were "made alive" in your spirit, there was one of you. Now there are two of you: *Old-you* "dead because of sin;"[39] and *New-you* "alive to God in Christ Jesus."[40]

God never confuses *New-you* with *Old-you*. He knows all about *Other-you, Fleshy-you, Bogus-you*. Though *Twin-you* may look identical to *You-you*, God can tell you apart. *E. Twin* was "sold into bondage to sin" long ago.[41] *Old-you* was already "dead in trespasses" before it came forth from your mother's womb.[42] *Old-nature, Used-to-be-the-only-you* was born of flesh . . . and it was cursed by Adam's disobedience.[43] The offspring of Adam (i.e. *his seed*) "all die,"[44] so there never was any hope for *Other-you* to reconcile with God.

That's why God formed a new people for Himself,[45] "a chosen race . . . a holy nation, a people for God's own possession" through the promise to Abraham.[46] God set apart the Father of faith and his offspring by declaring, "In your seed all the families of the earth shall be blessed" (i.e. uncursed).[47] Remember, God uses promises, not commandments, to secure people to Himself, and "the promises were spoken to Abraham and to his seed . . . that is, Christ."[48]

**That is the incredible, transformational change-everything promise. Since God's seed gave life to your spirit by faith,** *Born-again-you* **"cannot sin."**

As a believer in Christ, *New-you* was "born again not of seed which is perishable but imperishable, that is, through the living and enduring word of God."[49] By faith and through grace, *New-you, Spiritual-you* is a descendant of Abraham, "created in righteousness and holiness of the truth."[50] God's promise these thousands of years after Adam, Noah, Abraham, Moses, and Christ's appearing is that if you believe in Jesus, you become a child of God, "born, not of blood nor of the will of the flesh nor of the will of man, but of God."[51]

That is the incredible, transformational change-everything promise. Since God's seed gave life to your spirit by faith, *Born-again-you* "cannot sin."[52]

*Old-me* remains full of unrighteousness and death, and it will always be a sinner. But just as Jesus never sinned, neither does *New-me* because "it is no longer I [*Twin-me*] who lives, but Christ lives in *Me-me;* and the life which I now live in the flesh, I live by faith in the Son of God, who loved *New-me* and gave Himself up for *Me-me*."[53]

*Real-me. Forever-me. Never-to-sin-or-die-again-me.*

---

1   Galatians 3:24
2   John 4:42; 1 John 4:14
3   Titus 3:4-5
4   Titus 3:7
5   2 Timothy 1:9-10
6   Romans 1:25
7   1 Timothy 1:8-11
8   Romans 5:19-21
9   James 4:6; 1 Peter 5:5
10  Luke 5:31-32
11  John 9:39-41
12  See Mark 1:1-4
13  Matthew 5:18
14  Galatians 3:8
15  Hebrews 7:27; 9:13-14
16  Hebrews 9:26
17  Mark 1:4
18  Acts 5:31
19  Galatians 3:14
20  Galatians 4:1-7
21  Galatians 4:4-5
22  Romans 7:1-4
23  Psalm 51:3
24  Romans 7:15
25  Romans 6:13
26  Romans 7:19
27  Romans 7:14ff
28  Romans 7:15
29  Romans 7:18
30  Hebrews 10:26
31  1 John 3:9

32 Romans 7:15
33 Romans 7:17, 20
34 Romans 8:1
35 John 3:3, 5
36 Philippians 3:9
37 2 Corinthians 5:17
38 John 1:13; 1 Peter 1:23
39 Romans 8:10
40 Romans 6:11
41 Romans 7:14
42 Ephesians 2:1
43 John 3:6; Romans 5:18-19
44 1 Corinthians 15:22
45 Isaiah 43:21
46 Deuteronomy 7:6-8; 1 Peter 2:10
47 Genesis 22:18; Acts 3:25
48 Galatians 3:16
49 1 Peter 1:23
50 Ephesians 4:24
51 John 1:12-13
52 1 John 3:9
53 Galatians 2:20

# Chapter 13

# Good-Bye to the Dead, Old Guy

---

A s you suspected, something—someone—has been working against you to sabotage your earnest resolution to fully and obediently follow Jesus. *E. Twin* has several aliases. Or, should I say, the Bible uses various names for the evil side of us who splits our living space into two unequal parts. I say unequal because *Twin-me* outweighs *Me-me* by a considerable margin, as he has had more time to grow and develop. *Twin-me*, "with its passions and desires,"[1] is actively at work "in the members of our body to bear fruit for death."[2]

*Flesh* is perhaps the most familiar name for *Other-me*. Before we came to Christ, we were like Siamese Twins, joined together with *Flesh* from birth. One with it, "we lived in the lusts of the flesh, indulging the desires of the flesh."[3] In the joined-together condition, we shared the same fate as our twin—destined for the wrath that God pours out on "ungodliness and unrighteousness."[4] As the saying goes, we were as good as dead.

But when we received Christ as our Savior, God performed a profoundly spiritual operation to forever separate one twin from the other. "By the circumcision of Christ," a "circumcision made without hands,"[5] God severed *Flesh* from our spirit. It was an inner circumcision, "of the heart, by the Spirit, not by the letter."[6] God made us alive by grace.[7] Though *Flesh-you* is dead, *Spirit-you* lives, thanks to Christ's righteousness.[8] We have not just been "born of the flesh," but also "of the Spirit."[9]

As vigorously as you may wash and deodorize it, *Flesh* always reasserts its rancid and rank constitution. Like a long-dead body in a tomb, *Flesh* cannot be justified or counted innocent in God's eyes, no matter how virtuously it may be wrapped in "the works of the Law."[10]

*Flesh* is prolific and powerful—and not easily overcome. Like a ruthless crime boss, it takes perverse pleasure in trying to turn you crooked with bribes and threats; it defiles you by making you party to its murders, perversions, and addictions. It has a voracious appetite, wanting what it wants and insisting on being "indulged" in "corrupt desires."[11] *Flesh* couples with sin in every imaginable way, giving birth to offspring of jealousy, anger, idolatry, sensuality, dissension, factions and immorality, and other "deeds of the flesh."[12]

Occasionally, your evil twin (*E. Twin*) is also called the "old self."[13] That old nature is irredeemably infected by—and owes its only allegiance to—the *sin-force*.[14] *Old-self* didn't change when we got saved. *Old-self* embarrasses us like a peculiar relative or a sibling whose behavior we cannot control—no matter how we reason or threaten. We feel like hypocrites. Though *New-self* wants to turn over a new leaf, *Old-self* wants to live exactly like it did before.

Creation was "subjected to futility" and corruption when the *sin-force* infected the world,[15] and in the same way, *Old-self* (aka *Flesh*) is perpetually off-center and at odds with God's purposes. In fact, *E. Twin* helps the *sin-force* hijack the laws of God in our heart—perverting them from godly restraints on our behavior into "sinful passions" that stimulate wicked imaginings and activities.[16]

> **E. Twin helps the sin-force hijack the laws of God in our heart–perverting them from godly restraints on our behavior into "sinful passions."**

It pains and confuses us that daily decisions to live right aren't always easy or automatic. We find ourselves debating with—and sometimes listening to—*Old-self*. If we aren't careful and determined, *Old-self* runs amuck in and with our life. All believers have that struggle. *Old-self* keeps showing up when we least want it. Consciously and intentionally we must make the decision to "lay aside" *Old-self,* and "put on" *New-self.*[17]


**Flesh and Spirit**

Two-of-me. Two-of-you.

Because *Flesh* (in general) "sets its desire against the Spirit,"[18] the two of them, the *Two-of-us* fight one another constantly like Greco-Roman wrestlers.[19] Keeping *Old-me* in check is a life-long struggle requiring me to buffet my body many times each day. Even when I spot the warning signs that beefy *Flesh* is growing restless and hungry, I have a hard time preventing it from breaking out of the mental and physical restraints I put on it. Though I try to "discipline my body" for godliness,[20] I do not always succeed. *Old-me* dominates *New-me* too much of the time—and that distresses me deeply. I'm sure it grieves you, too.

Wouldn't it be a dream-come-true if all your impulses and desires were Christ-centered and righteous? Imagine what it would be like to be set free from your body of "sinful flesh."[21] If you didn't need to drag your physical frame around and overcome its reluctance to obey God, wouldn't that be fabulous? Of course, that's what we look forward to in Heaven. But the point I want to register is that as much as *New-you* wants *Old-you* to weaken and surrender, so *Flesh* works every angle and takes every opportunity to enfeeble and exhaust *Spiritual-you.* The battle is joined.

*Flesh-you* wants *New-you* dead. It cannot succeed, of course, in killing *New-you.* Satan, the *sin-force,* and *Flesh-you* conspire against *Spiritual-you,* but they lost the "power of death" over your spirit when Christ died in your stead.[22]

> **Satan, the *sin-force,* and *Flesh-you* conspire against *Spiritual-you,* but they lost the "power of death" over your spirit when Christ died in your stead.**

## Sowing and Reaping

Knowing it cannot end your spirit-life, *Old-you* tries to at least weaken you, so that you will not make much of a difference in the lives of people around you. *New-you* is a total threat to *Old-you*—and all its evil-spirited kind—so *Old-you* employs an unusual strategy to keep you off-balance and spiritually ineffective. The best way I can explain it is for you to picture a three-legged race: *New-you* and *Old-you* are tied together, one leg each, and the rules say all three legs must move toward the finish line together.

*Old-you* wants to get really, really fat—so grossly overweight and out-of-shape that *New-you* finds it impossibly difficult to drag its partner toward the finish line. *Flesh-you* knows it cannot prevent *Spiritual-you* from eventually being freed of its carnal counterpart.

When you die, the cord that connects you with *Flesh* gets cut, and *New-you* will be clothed in a heavenly body. But in the meantime, *Flesh-you* wants to halt your forward progress with intriguing offers and suggestions.

> **What we sow, we reap. If we plant seeds of corn, the field doesn't sprout barley.**

*Spiritual-you* submits to the Law of God, but *Flesh-you* serves sin.[23] That's why it is so dangerous to follow *Flesh's* desires. The decision we must make over and over is where will we invest ourselves: will we sow to the spirit or sow to the flesh?

What we sow, we reap. If we plant seeds of corn, the field doesn't sprout barley. That basic equation was woven into Creation from the very beginning when God established fruit containing "seed in them, after their kind."[24] Grace does not set aside such pre-Law rulings of Creation. When we "sow to the flesh,"[25] we suffer loss at some dimension for those wrongs —even if we don't realize it.

*Flesh* tempts, lures, and tricks us in all the wrong directions. And we sin. We covet, rage, fear, lie, and hate. We judge others and pity ourselves. We grow embittered, impatient, and self-seeking—and temporarily lose the struggle. Again.

Grace and the Law don't differ over right and wrong. The deep disagreement between *legalism* and Grace is their counsel for how to eliminate the wrong. When we do wrong, the *Spirit of the Pharisee* pounces on us with shame and fearful guilt. *See,* it sneers, *You do not have God's Spirit inside of you because you give into fleshly desires.*

God isn't like that. His Spirit says, *Yes, your sins are trying to kill you, but they will not overcome you, for I am with you to deliver you.*[26]

The *Spirit of the Pharisee* does not accept *Two-me* people. It insists that any effort to attain righteousness must be accomplished by *Old-me, Twin-me, Flesh-me* working harder to discipline wayward impulses. The Spirit of God, on the other hand, offers to purge those urges from our heart—before they sprout into actions.


## Sanctification

It is difficult to explain the spiritual process the Spirit uses to aid our struggle against *Flesh.* Theologians call it sanctification—the progressive increase of good and obedience in our lives. Perhaps an analogy of a field or garden will help. The Spirit crowds out flesh-seeds in our heart by planting spirit-seeds; over time, those seeds produce "fruit of the Spirit" that leave little room for sinful desires to grow. Spirit-sown seeds of righteousness are effective in slowing down and preventing the growth of flesh-sown sin-seeds.

Fruit like "love, joy, peace, patience, kindness, goodness, faithfulness, gentleness, self-control,"[27] amend our behavior toward others not because we're obeying a list of commands, but because we've had a change of heart. There is no provision in the Law of Moses for the growth of such internal fruit.[28] The Law primarily focuses on instruction for physical worship toward God and external behavior toward other people. It has little bearing on what God, by His Spirit, accomplishes inside of us.

People under a legalistic mindset wrongly assume that the goal for our lives is to become righteous—on our own. God certainly does not want us to give place to flesh lusts; He wants us to be holy in all our behavior, just as He is holy.[29] But He has a different plan than we do for our righteousness. God offers us a heart transplant—replacing a "stony heart" that beats disobediently, with a soft heart that keeps rhythm with His.[30]

*Legalism* puts the burden on us, and our own-effort obedience. It barks at us like a frustrated foreman toward a new worker, "I've told you what to do. What's your problem?" The Holy Spirit also instructs us, but He offers to remind us as many times as necessary; He willingly helps us learn how to do what we're supposed to do by pointing out where and how we're still doing it incorrectly. The Holy Spirit leads us into obedience; He doesn't just command us and leave us on our own to

> **God offers us a heart transplant–replacing a "stony heart" that beats disobediently, with a soft heart that keeps rhythm with His.**

obey. He wants us to get it right in the end; the *Spirit of the Pharisee* simply wants our audition for the job to end.

## Obedience

Let me say again, I'm not telling you to disregard the commandments. I have spent most of this book trying to encourage you with how boundless God's love and grace are for you. But sin and disobedience have tremendous power to affect your life-on-earth. God would not have given us commandments if we were free to live any way we wanted to live—without consequences. God chastened Saul after he disobeyed God's commands concerning the Amelekites: "To obey is better than sacrifice . . . Rebellion is as the sin of divination."[31] In simple language, God was telling Saul that disobedience moves us toward a different future than the one God has in mind for us.

After experiencing God's mercy,[32] we want to turn our life over to His purposes. Obedience is living as He wants us to live, refusing to be shaped by the world. We ought to offer our bodies as "living and holy" sacrifices to God.[33] That surrender, to "live the rest of the time in the flesh no longer for the lusts of men, but for the will of God,"[34] is our "spiritual service of worship."[35]

But a list of rules and regulations, without the inner working of the Holy Spirit, will only improve your behavior. It will not develop you into a spiritually mature person. Reformed *Flesh*, disciplined *Flesh*, less-wild-than-it-was-before-*Flesh* is still *Flesh*, and no amount of rehabilitation changes its fundamental nature. If we do the work ourselves, and attempt to man-handle *Flesh* with our own efforts, we will accomplish no more than Sarah and Abraham accomplished through Hagar. *Flesh* only begets flesh.

Remember, God advances His Kingdom by faith in His promises.[36] So, when it comes to our wayward conduct, we should look for His promise. The promise of God, as it relates to our behavior, is that if we walk by the Spirit, we will "not carry out the desire of the flesh."[37] The Holy Spirit Himself works to undermine our wicked thoughts, and veto the vote of our flesh. The Holy Spirit inspires our obedience. Our weak efforts to resist sin will be fortified with "His power, which mightily works within [us]."[38]

**Obeying comes more from listening attentively to the Spirit's instruction than from striving relentlessly.**

We aren't fighting this battle alone. *God-With-Us* will save us from our sins.[39] The Holy Spirit applies God's word at the point of our deep infection, just like radiation treatment targets cancer cells. At "the division of soul and spirit,"[40] where the malignant sin-tumor metastasizes and spreads sinful thoughts into every area of our life, the Holy Spirit combats the *sin-force* with God's laws.[41] An internal witness replaces external standards. Obeying comes more from listening attentively to the Spirit's instruction than from striving relentlessly.

The One who wrote His laws for holiness on stone is the One who now works inside us, "both to will and to work for His good pleasure."[42] If He could get His Law into our world eons ago, He certainly knows how to get His Law into our lives. The *Spirit of the Pharisee* does not want you to trust the work of God in your life—or in others'.

Even though God, Himself, is challenging, convicting, and changing you from the inside out, *legalism* still insists that you need to assist God's inner work in your soul with works inspired by the Law of Moses. That is like saying in order to get correct dimensions of an object you hold in your hand, you need to measure its shadow.


## The Athens Liar

The angry prophet who accosted me in Athens wanted me to condemn my friends—and tell them God's judgment was coming to punish their sin. That was and is a lie formulated by our defeated adversary and proclaimed by evil-spirited beings that oppose true righteousness. The false dogma espoused by the *Spirit of the Pharisee* suggests that Christians must be sinless in order to retain God's favor, and when believers "fall into sin," they fall from Grace—to face the judgment of God.

> **Born-again, redeemed, and on-their-way-to-Heaven people like us get taken prisoner by the very evil we hate in our life.**

The truth is that even the most sincere follower of Christ will struggle with—and sometimes lose the tug-of-war against—*Flesh*. Born-again, redeemed, and on-their-way-to-Heaven people like us get taken prisoner by the very evil we hate in our life. Though we joyfully agree with and serve the Law of God in our inner person, a different law continues to animate *Old-self*.[43] *Old-self* obeys its master (sin), even though *New-self* struggles against sin's mastery.

Sometimes *E. Twin* resembles me so closely, even I cannot tell us apart. That is exactly why Paul cried out in frustration, *Who will set me free from Old-me? I feel like a prisoner to myself. Can't someone disconnect me "from the body of this death?"*[44]

The Law cannot distinguish between *Old-self* and *New-self.* But God can. By the Grace of God, *Old-me* "died with Christ" on the Cross; *New-me* lives with Christ, never to die again.[45] God's Spirit cultivates spirit-seeds in *New-me*, while also weeding out works of *Flesh*. Though *Old-me* is completely sinful, I am completely freed from judgment, guilt, and condemnation through Jesus Christ because He made *New-me* completely sinless.[46]

It wouldn't be so complicated and confusing if *Old-me* and *New-me* didn't look alike and have the same name.

## The Bill Collector

I concluded the three-night lecture in Athens with my favorite image—a vignette that speaks reassuringly to me personally when I hear the accusations of guilt slung at my soul. Even armed with mounds of theological evidence and Scripture verses, I still scuffle with the *Spirit of the Pharisee* and encounter ambushes of condemnation. This picture of the Bill Collector and me, as a new tenant in an apartment, makes me smile—and thank Jesus, again.

Imagine that you have just moved into a new apartment. Strangely enough, the previous tenant, who passed away just a few weeks earlier, had exactly the same name as you—first, last, and middle. You didn't even need to change the name on the lobby mailbox. While you are still unpacking the boxes in your new place, someone knocks on the door. You open it, and a very official-looking man with a clipboard claims to be confirming certain financial records. Quickly, you size him up and realize he's some sort of a bounty-hunter doing repo work.

He asks your name with feigned politeness, and with a nod of his head, ticks a box next to your printed name and address. "Yes, that matches our records," he says aloud—but mostly to himself.

"I have a copy of an overdue account," he announces while unclipping and unfolding several sheets of itemized purchases to hold up for your inspection. You see your name and address . . . and the payment due: $14,086,993.

You protest vehemently, "I don't know what to say. I don't have that kind of money. And that isn't my bill. I never bought any of the items listed here."

The Bill Collector merely repeats your name and address, reading it off the invoice, as though daring you to exclaim that isn't your name and address. The Bill Collector thinks himself quite clever for tricking you into admitting who you are before disclosing your debt. He's sure he has the right name and address.

Then it strikes you, and you almost start laughing in relief: "Ha. This is amazing. The guy who lived here before me—he had the exact same name as me. Those charges must be his, and I'm glad I'm not him. Wow, what a scare . . ."

Just before you shut the door and return to your unpacked boxes, you add as an afterthought, "By the way, you are going to have some difficulty collecting your money. Not only does he not live here anymore, he's dead. So, good luck, buster!"

I've lost count of how many times that guilt-bearing Bill Collector has come knocking at my door; he likely will for the rest of my life. Yours, too.

His knocking sometimes lasts for several days, as he hopes to shame us into answering his summons. The pounding unsettles us. To get our attention, the *Spirit of the Pharisee* hires shouting prophets like the man in Athens, who threaten us with legal proceedings if we don't settle our account immediately. That demon has other tricks to get us to own up to our debt: it offers to "forgive" several of the disputed charges so that the total is only $11.2 million; it proposes installment plans with small, regular payments; it bargains for IOUs, debtor's prison, and even accepts depression and despair as positive first-steps toward an eventual settlement.

I feel better prepared for him now than I was when I arrived in Greece and was accosted in the church parking lot. But I must acknowledge I'm still getting used to the fact that *New-Me* and *Old-me* aren't the same me. It is hard to believe, just like it was hard for Abraham to imagine that his old body could sire a child. But he chose to believe, and God "reckoned his faith as righteousness."[47]

By faith, I am a "child of Abraham," and I believe Christ condemned the sin that would have condemned me; He put to death the death that would have killed me.[48]

> **By faith, I am a "child of Abraham," and I believe Christ condemned the sin that would have condemned me; He put to death the death that would have killed me.**

God's grace-and-judgment separated me from my uncleanness, so I wouldn't die in it.[49] God preserved *Real-me* through baptism like He preserved Noah through the Flood.[50] *Two-me* has undergone spiritual circumcision, and my "body of sin" (aka *E. Twin*) was "done away with" like the fleshy fold.[51] *Old-me* was crucified with Christ—and died. *New-me* has risen from the grave, never again to die as penalty for sin.[52] *Real-me* is totally "freed from sin."[53]

The Bill Collector will pound at your door with condemnation when your sins become too monstrous or too numerous. He will insist that you are disqualified from God's never-ending grace because you continued to sin; he'll say you didn't do enough for Christ, after He did so much for you. When the heavy, anxious awareness of your sin threatens to smother you, try doing what I do: Shout back, "The sin and guilt aren't mine. They belong to the old-man who used to live here. He died."

I am not going to assume the debt for some dead, old guy just because he has my name.

---

1. Galatians 5:24
2. Romans 7:5
3. Ephesians 2:3
4. Romans 1:18
5. Colossians 2:11
6. Romans 2:29
7. Ephesians 2:4-5
8. Romans 8:9-10

9   John 3:5-8; Romans 8:8-9
10  Romans 3:20
11  2 Peter 2:10
12  Galatians 5:19-21
13  Romans 6:6; Ephesians 4:22; Colossians 3:9
14  Romans 7:18, 23, 25
15  Romans 8:20-21
16  Romans 7:5ff
17  Ephesians 4:22-24; Colossians 3:9-10
18  Galatians 5:17
19  Galatians 5:17
20  1 Corinthians 9:27; 1 Timothy 4:7
21  Romans 8:3
22  Acts 2:22-24; 1 Corinthians 15:54-57; Hebrews 2:14-15
23  Romans 7:25
24  Genesis 1:11-12
25  Galatians 6:8
26  Jeremiah 1:8, 19
27  Galatians 5:22
28  Galatians 5:23
29  1 Peter 1:14-15
30  Ezekiel 36:26
31  1 Samuel 15:22-23
32  Romans 11:30
33  Romans 12:1
34  1 Peter 4:2
35  Romans 12:1
36  1 Timothy 1:4
37  Galatians 5:16
38  Colossians 1:29
39  Matthew 1:23
40  Hebrews 4:12
41  Jeremiah 31:33
42  Philippians 2:13
43  Romans 7:20ff
44  Romans 7:22-24
45  Romans 6:8
46  John 3:16-18
47  Genesis 15:6; James 2:23
48  Romans 8:3
49  Leviticus 15:31
50  1 Peter 3:18-22
51  Colossians 2:11
52  John 11:26; Romans 6:8-9; 1 Peter 2:24
53  Romans 6:6-7

also from
**DR. DANIEL A. BROWN**

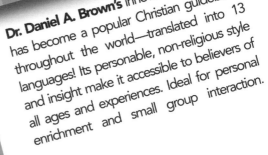